VOICES: MODERNITY AND ITS DISCONTENTS

First published in 1987 by:
Spokesman
Bertrand Russell House
Gamble Street
Nottingham, England
Tel. 0602 708318

and 171 First Avenue, Atlantic Highlands,
New Jersey 07716, USA
for The Hobo Press

British Library Cataloguing in Publication Data

Modernity and its discontents. — (Voices).
1. Political science
I. Bourne, Bill   II. Eichler, Udi
III. Series
320   JA71

ISBN 0-85124-472-6
ISBN 0-85124-482-3 Pbk

Printed by the Russell Press Ltd, Nottingham
(Tel. 0602 784505)

VOICES

from the Channel 4 Television series

MODERNITY AND ITS
DISCONTENTS

Saul Bellow	Ulrich Briefs
Martin Amis	Ralf Dahrendorf
Ernest Gellner	Alan Touraine
Charles Taylor	Octavio Paz
Christopher Lasch	Leszek Kolakowski
Cornelius Castoriadis	Johan Galtung
Daniel Bell	Immanuel Wallerstein
Emma Rothschild	Anthony Giddens

Michael Ignatieff

EDITED BY Bill Bourne, Udi Eichler and David Herman

SPOKESMAN
Nottingham: Atlantic Highlands

in association with
THE HOBO PRESS

Contents

Introduction   7

1. The Moronic Inferno   11
   Saul Bellow, Martin Amis

2. The Tough and the Tender   26
   Ernest Gellner, Charles Taylor

3. The Culture of Narcissism   42
   Christopher Lasch, Cornelius Castoriadis

4. The Post-Industrial Society   57
   David Bell, Emma Rothschild, Ulrich Briefs

5. The New Politics   75
   Ralf Dahrendorf, Alan Touraine

6. Lost Illusions   90
   Octavio Paz, Leszek Kolakowski

7. Living in the Interregnum   102
   Johan Galtung, Immanuel Wallerstein, Anthony Giddens

Moderator: Michael Ignatieff

Introduction

Voices is a television oddity. Apparently set in a late-night Oriental carpet warehouse, it attempts to present the most exciting debates going on in the world of ideas. The debates may be topical (The New Cold War, The Future of Work) or timeless (The Mind/Brain Argument). The important thing is that they matter and deserve to reach the large audience that only television can provide.

This means going into often new and foreign terrain. New because our world is rapidly changing. Issues like Artificial Intelligence and The Post-Industrial Society are now upon us, transforming the world we live in. Developments in computer technology pose real and disturbing questions about the mind and what it means to be human. This doesn't mean taking some 'Gee Wiz' attitude to the new, but to think through the changes and find the voices who can make sense of this newly emerging landscape.

The humanities too have undergone tremendous upheavals in the last 20 years: new ideas, new uncertainties and even new subjects. The language of literary critics and historians is sometimes barely recognisable and has moved away from our own common sense and everyday assumptions about writing or the past. There has been a revolution in the world of criticism, undermining our older assumptions about knowledge and the self. Increasingly it is here in the world of ideas rather than in the arts, that we sense The Shock of The New.

Much of this shock is muffled by parochialism, distancing ourselves from new work by seeing it as faddish and foreign. Because so many of the great creative thinkers come from across the Atlantic or the Channel they lack any regular access to our review-pages or TV screens, we tend to lose touch with the most important debates going on elsewhere. The important voices from abroad go unheard as if what they have to say doesn't matter. The results can be comical. When the British press finally caught up with Structuralist ideas during the row in the Cambridge English Department a few years ago, it was easy to forget that the theories at the centre of the controversy had been commonplace in Paris for 20 years. Despite the talk about 'The Global Village' intellectuals like Chomsky or Levi-Straus remain strangers to our screens and their ideas remain at the margin of our culture. Even more extraordinary is how rare it is on British television to find discussion of the work of British intellectuals like Edward Thompson, John Berger and Raymond Williams. There is no obvious forum for the discussion of their ideas, at a time when British intellectual culture is in fact very rich.

This is part of a growing problem of communication. Our culture has created a huge gulf between its thinkers and the rest. We take this for granted in the more arcane reaches of science and mathematics, but the same is happening in literary criticism and history and the growing areas where science touches our lives. Both academics and media have been notoriously bad at communicating the main intellectual developments of our time to the rest of us, so that like Miss Havisham we continue to live in the past, surrounded by out-of-date theories and cobwebbed assumptions.

This in turn is partly a matter of categories. Some of these debates are neither Arts, Philosophy or Science in any clear sense, but slip in between established categories. When Umberto Eco and Stuart Hall talk about a pervasive sense of crisis — is that Current Affairs? Politics? History? When Cornelius Castoriadis and Chistopher Lasch talk about the breakdown of a sense of community or belonging they are not just talking about politics or sociology. These discussions are about culture in the largest sense, issues which speak to the heart of our experience, but which have no obvious home in the universities or the media.

Voices, then, tries to be alert to these problems, to this need for a forum where these kinds of issues can be discussed, and to follow an agenda which is being set by writers and intellectuals here and abroad. This agenda is often new and foreign, and may have no clear signposts. And even where there are signposts (Post-Structuralism, Post-Modernism) the question is what do they mean and why do they matter? That is perhaps a fancy way of saying: Who are the most interesting voices of our age and what do they have to say to us?

The discussions that follow set out to answer a puzzling question: Why do people living in the most affluent and dynamic societies the world has ever known seem so worried about the present, and so frightened of the future? What is it that we find so troubling about life in the modern world?

One answer that recurs through these discussions is *Change*. The social, political and economic landscape seems to be changing fast, so fast that some speak of a profound historical shift comparable with the Industrial Revolution or the end of the Middle Ages. There are different names for this sense of transition — The Post-Industrial Society, Post-Modernity, Late Capitalism — and very different views of what it is that is coming to an end. But together they make up a debate about 'Modernity and Its Discontents' which is now going on throughout the world of ideas.

Voices has been a regular annual feature of Channel 4 since November 1982. The programme is made by Brook Productions and produced by Udi Eichler and David Herman.

CHAPTER 1

The Moronic Inferno

Michael Ignatieff
with Saul Bellow & Martin Amis

Ignatieff: The characters in Saul Bellow's novels all seem to be saying with a mixture of horror and fascination, 'what's the world coming to?' For the next seven weeks on *Voices* that's going to be our subject too. Why do people living in the most affluent and dynamic societies the world has ever known seem so worried about the present, so frightened of the future? Why does the social, political and economic landscape seem to be changing so fast? What is the world coming to? Saul Bellow is a perfect starting point because this is his subject. Over 40 years he's described the loss of a whole cultural tradition, not just of books and ideas but of human qualities and feelings, of community and dignity which find no echo in the contemporary capitals of America. Familiar landmarks are missing in Bellow's words, but his books make clear how important those landmarks are to us, how they help to keep us human. They're part of a cultural tradition going back hundreds of years, and without those landmarks we're lost in what he calls 'the moronic inferno.' A younger generation is drawn precisely by this sense of the infernal in American culture. Martin Amis, better than any, conveys the fascination and weird richness of the culture of *Playboy* fantasies and space invaders in a book of essays he happens to have called *The Moronic Inferno.* Both writers are here tonight to discuss with me just what the world is coming to, and to ponder whether the voyage we're on from Herzog to Hefner is a journey of no return. I thought we should start with this business of the moronic inferno, the sense of the infernal in modern culture, the sense that it's a *moronic* inferno. I'm just wondering what you meant when you picked up that phrase, which I think is from Wyndham Lewis, if I'm right.

Bellow: That's right.

Ignatieff: Just what it means to you, what it's conveying.

Bellow: Well, it means a chaotic state which no one has sufficient internal organisation to resist, and in which one is overwhelmed by all kinds of powers, political, technological, military, economic and so on, which carry everything before them with a kind of heathen disorder in which we're supposed to survive with all our human qualities. And whether this is possible or not is the question we're addressing, I suppose.

Ignatieff: What is this lack of a centre? You seem to be implying that if somehow we could have a different kind of self, a more resolute self, we could withstand this onslaught of forces a little better. What do you mean?

Bellow: Well it doesn't need to be a different kind of self. It needs to be a self however. That is to say, one witnesses the obliteration of true forms of individuality in this scene. And the reason why writers are writers, if they are authentic writers, is that they do confront the scene with a fairly well organised individuality. I don't know whether Martin would agree or disagree with this.

Ignatieff: Yes, you've picked up the term 'moronic inferno' and you've also talked a lot about the self. I'm wondering how you see the forces confronting the self at the moment.

Amis: Well, as Saul says, I think it probably comes down to our valuation of human life has along the way become thinner, or more nebulous. We don't quite give it the credit it once had. And once that goes or starts to go, then the whole nature of reality becomes something much more unreliable. There are many forces at work.

Ignatieff: What are they, Martin?

Amis: Well, it seems that the world has become much more politicised in a woolly way. This, for instance, means that anger is allowed onto the political scene as a, not legitimate or legal, but accepted part of geopolitical life and, more locally, certain sorts of insurrection. I often thought, during the rioting recently and in 1981, that that itself was a sort of criminals' lib, in a sense. In that, you know, we're just criminals. We want to be self-respecting like anyone else, we want to get on with our job. Why are we being singled out for persecution by the forces of law and order? An imbalance seems to have been struck.

Ignatieff: So we're talking about some very crucial thinning of our humanity in the face of the moronic inferno, the onslaught both of terror, media, news, the constant kind of cycle of violence we're exposed to. I'm just wondering how one puts examples to this thinning of humanity that both of you are picking up. I mean, what examples are in your mind when you say that?

Bellow: Well you go back to the places where you lived in earlier times and you see that they're in total decay. And you see that the reconstructed Chicago along the lake shore is a sort of sanctuary, in which you live under a kind of feudal protection of moats and TV surveillance and all the rest of that. You don't go out. There is no natural life of the streets any more. And that's very hard to take, you know, because, to use the American word, socialisation of that sort has stopped, except in certain protected bars and so on. But all of it — people live with it. They don't even acknowledge how terrible it's become, they internalise all of this, and they congratulate themselves for having avoided being murdered in the streets as if that were due to some skill of theirs, you know. It's just an accident. And if you'll allow me to turn theoretical for a moment — part of me is a college professor, unhappily — I'd like to say that this word that's become so popular, 'charisma', introduced by Max Weber, who got, I think, most of the idea from Nietzsche, charisma had some sort of religious meaning. But now violence has become charisma. That is to say the criminals are charismatic, and people feel 'yes, yes, it's right that they should do this,' because of the charisma.

Ignatieff: But what I don't focus on clearly is that there is that sense, when you ask the question 'what is going on?' what is certainly going on is terror and violence, and it scares the hell out of everybody who looks at it. But if you look in another perspective, and this is where it's so difficult to figure these things out, we are the most — I'm talking about the Western democracies — the most institutionalised, humane societies the world has ever known. I put it badly, but I mean we take care of people in ways that would be the envy of the 17th and 18th century, and yet both of you are saying our sense of humanity is thinning out. Now, I can't sort this paradox out. I mean, how do we cut into it? Do we just have charismatic lunatics on the one hand and, you know, very good childcare, a decent welfare state, a society with all its failings that is trying to put a value on human life, do we just have them in one compartment and the other thing in the other? I mean, how do we put these things together?

Amis: Well, there is one great underlying uncertainty, and we now find ourselves, for instance, at this moment, having the fate of the earth in the hands of, on the one hand, an old actor, and on the other, a prison warden. I get a great sense of discrepancy from that. That is what the world has come to. And surely we are living in the most dangerous era that the human species has ever gone through, without compare. But I think that this has been — Nadezhda Mandelstam called it the 'fractricidal century', but it's the suicidal century too. I mean, there is this threat. It would be extraordinary if we didn't react to it in violent ways, I think, to this central discrepancy.

Ignatieff: So there's some sense in your mind that the menace of collective suicide is one of the things that in turn makes us violent, makes us careless with life in some sense. Is that what you're saying?

Amis: I think it's bound to declass ourselves in our own eyes. I mean, Saul Bellow often talks in his novels about being human in fact not being a given, that it's something you have to work at, it's a privilege. And the humanistic culture that we all feel is losing its grip on life was one of those nutrients.

Ignatieff: Let's just pick up one thing that Martin is saying there, which is the sense that the whole context now is the context of nuclear war, and that that is, as you put it very well, declassing us in some sense. That we're more careless of life in some mysterious sense as a consequence of that. You would have thought we'd care much more passionately about life in that context.

Bellow: Well what you said earlier is quite true. That is to say the democratic societies of the West feel obligated to take care of the young, the sick, the needy, the aged and so on, and this is certainly a laudable thing. But of course it has no personal dimension, it's all done in a bureaucratic way, so that people can tell themselves 'I voted for Congressman so-and-so who voted for the Great Society programme and therefore I'm in the clear myself. I am not only a nice, decent, well brought-up and prosperous person, but I'm for all the good things and I'm against all the bad things.' But there is nothing personal about this. That is to say, it happens bureaucratically and it happens through all kinds of government agencies, and it happens without any sort of care for persons, only for categories of persons. And this, I think, is one of the problems.

Ignatieff: So what you have there is putting a very different spin on the ball I sent you, which is to say 'yes, we're a caring society but it's a sort of institutionalised care that kind of disconnects people so that their common humanity is somehow not reinforced by that process.'

Bellow: It's the kind of care which enables the individual to get rid of the problem for himself, because it's being taken care of. Science is taking care of it, experts are taking care of it, social workers and psychologists are taking care of it. Of course they're making a damn mess of the whole thing. And the effect finally of all of this caring is also dehumanising. One can see that with the American welfare population.

Ignatieff: Let's broaden this frame a little. We're talking about a very scary public world out there. You're talking about after 6 o'clock at night you read your newspapers and you don't go downstairs onto the street because it's a scary world. Aren't we looking at here the decay of the public realm? I mean, it seems to me a recurring concern in your novels for a kind of civic world in which strangers can be together in public places in which they can act politically together. How have we lost that? Is it just so simple as saying we've got a scary underclass on the street? Surely there must be something much more to the decay of the public world than that?

Bellow: Well I suppose there is. And I'm not so sure that the public world has altogether decayed. I think in many ways it's

supplanted the private world. When people spend 50 hours a week
sitting before the television set, that means that the TV set is the
master of the house. It has replaced family life and family authority.
Otherwise why would everybody be looking at the set? In other
words, it means it's an impoverishment of personal resources which
turns people outward.

Amis: Also, large areas of American life are organised around
television: politics, religion, sports. American lawyers are very well
schooled in soap operas so that they behave like the good guy. And
this again turns everything on its head.

Ignatieff: You've written very perceptively about the television
culture, Martin. I'm just wondering whether you share this view of
Saul Bellow's which seems to me very interesting, which is that the
public realm of television is kind of colonising and dominating the
private world, and the problem is not the decay of the public world
but a sense that the private world is disintegrating in the face of
television. Do you see it that way?

Amis: Well, no, I think it's at least as much a cause as a symptom.
I think one thing we haven't mentioned is the embarrassing
deterioration of our leaders. No longer do Cabinet meetings break
up while everyone hurries home to finish their translation of the
Aeneid, that doesn't happen any more. One of the embarrassing
things that these characters are now wishing on us is that they are
using television, they are beginning to use television. Of course,
America knows all about this. We're just beginning to use it, our
leaders. And watching Margaret Thatcher speak now in this sort of
trained way, half acting, what is she doing? She's not reading a
speech, she's not acting, she's doing something in between. I part
company with someone like that, they have stepped onto a different
channel of reality for me. And television isn't a symptom of that.

Ignatieff: It's an actual cause.

Amis: It's an agent.

Ignatieff: Do you agree?

Bellow: Well of course it is. I agree. I agree. I have some small
agreement with you too, though, because I feel that of course this
represents a borderline or terminating condition for civilisation as a
whole, and that the old forms of existence have worn out, so to
speak, and the new ones have not yet appeared and that people are
prospecting, as it were, in the desert for new forms. Television is in
part an expression of that. It is at the same time, however, very
powerful and manipulative and the media managers have
manipulative ends of their own, or ends for which they manipulate.

Ignatieff: That last remark, embedded in it was a very strong
image 'prospecting in the desert' for the new forms, the new way.
I'm just wondering, if you look back over your own — you've lived

this century very intensely — I'm just wondering, as you look back over it what are some of the new forms that seem definitely a harbinger of the new. Let's put television aside.

Bellow: Well, there's a kind of crazy process of emancipation going on. People are emancipating themselves from all kinds of things. Some bad, mostly good. Now, what that's going to lead to, I don't know. It depends really on the power of the imagination and its real root within. Because if you don't find a root within you're just gonna have these made-up things everywhere, you're gonna be surrounded by them.

Ignatieff: The new. So much of the new you've been greeting with a mixture of kind of astonishment and a kind of disgust, but there must be a kind of 'the new', prospecting in the desert you must have turned up a few gold nuggets in your pan, Martin.

Amis: Well, I think one thing that remains very strong in people, however debased, is the idea of art, even in the form of self-mutilation or self-decoration. If you look at the punks you see that they are people who have, as it were, sprayed themselves with graffiti. They've sort of vandalised themselves. But nonetheless it's all done with an idea of making something attractive or interesting. I think that is imperishable at least. But Christ knows what forms it will take.

Ignatieff: (to Bellow) Now, to allow you to become a college professor again, this public world, to call television the public world would surprise Aristotle. I mean, what the public realm meant to the whole classical tradition of politics was meeting in the forum to act together as citizens. Now civic courage is a phrase that recurs again and again in one of your books, I remember, a sense that what we need now is a little common, plain civic courage. Now that relates to that Aristotelian conception of the public and what did you mean — ?

Bellow: Well, we're a long way from Athens. Let's not kid ourselves about that.

Ignatieff: But have we lost it forever?

Bellow: Well I don't know what we've lost forever. All I can see is that certain things are happening and that these facts are perhaps exaggerated because I was manifested suddenly out of the middle ages, so to speak. As one of my wives used to say, 'you have a feudal character.' Well, maybe I did. It's perfectly true, it's possible that I did.

Ignatieff: I want to return both of you to your novels, in a way, because I think this will help us to widen out this framework. One of the things that interests me most about your characters, Saul Bellow, I mean when you think of Herzog, Sammler, Humboldt, Cord, these big, solid, very passionate men who all seem embarrassed by their saturation in a European culture which they often think has no purchase on the tough world of America. Now what I want to pick up there is that they're profoundly divided, they think on the one hand that what they care about most is Proust and Rilke, and on the other hand they think 'this has no purchase at all on the tough world of Lasalle Street, Chicago or New York.' I sense that ambivalence, the sense that they love that old culture and they sense it just doesn't connect to the world. I'm just wondering how you live that ambivalence, because I sense both of you live that.

Amis: I think what has made for a lot of confusion is that Saul Bellow in some of his novels, and me in mine, we are partly comic writers, and this has to be our material, and it's bound to look pretty odd, I think, when you put into a comic novel something that only used to be in comedy to be overthrown. I mean, comedy has a nice symmetrical shape, it corresponds to the smile on the mask, that you start off at a certain point, you enter complication, you emerge at the end. New relationships are formed, the old society is bested in some way. But one of the things, one of the many strange things that have happened in this century is that the genres are, their shape has gone and you're taking other things to laugh at. It's not just folly and pretension, the old butts of comedy, but murder.

Ignatieff: And rape.

Amis: And crime.

Ignatieff: Terror.

Amis: Yes. And it's bound to look pretty odd and look as though you are more fascinated by it than you are.

Ignatieff: What I hear Martin saying, there may be something that you feel as well, that the comic form — since I think you see yourself as a kind of comic writer — is a way of mastering this attraction/repulsion, this ambivalence, this sense that what one has to talk about is something very terrible, with equipment from an old culture which may not fit. Is that what the comic does, in a sense, in your work?

Bellow: Well I don't really know what it does because it's intuitive with me. So I don't tamper with it. But I think it has something to do with the fact that the protagonists are so often atypical, which makes them funny. And then of course they examine the typical and they find that is a comic gap.

Ignatieff: Yes. What is their atypicality, because that's what I was driving at?

Bellow: Well, they are literate, they've had some sort of education. Not just an education but one that has dedicated them to certain values which they're stuck with. And they're stuck with them in the sense that when they're up against persons in authority there's absolutely nothing they can do about it. There's a scene in

Humboldt's Gift, for instance, in which Charlie Citrine in Judges' Chambers want to turn into a King Lear, you know, and make an outcry about the way he's being brutalised.

Ignatieff: And it just isn't appropriate, to say the least.

Bellow: Well, if he says it they'll put him in a nuthouse. I mean, if he cries out, does the Lear on the heath scene, he's bound for the funny farm.

Amis: And in that scene, the two lawyers who have the marvellous names of Tomchek and Pinsker talk to Citrine with their breath 'rich in male hormones' and within a 'sour tang of male hormones', and they are presented as terrifically powerful and frightening men. And they are just holding back from saying to Citrine, you know, 'where do you get off with this culture? We're the realists and you'd better understand that.'

Ignatieff: It seems to me that something's changed in the hunger for education over your own lifetime, and I'm just wondering whether you could talk a little bit about that, going back to your first experiences.

Bellow: Well, you know, I think immigrant society in America made children very eager to find out what it was all about, get out on the streets and get away from what they called the ethnic atmosphere and so on, which people now cling to and are proud of. Certain immigrant groups didn't do it at all, they had their own parochial schools and spoke Czech or Polish or whatever it was. But we were turned out on the streets to make our own way in the twenties. In other words, the responsibility for your education was your own. And really it describes the formation of a soul, to pick your way. And it never stops. As Martin Amis said to me before, it never can stop, you have to go on with it and it requires a very special effort which most people are not prepared to make nowadays.

Ignatieff: Martin, that's one description of the education of a soul from one generation, how does it look from another generation?

Amis: I think the distractions are more, the demands on one's attention are more. I mean the technology of distracting you is far advanced. I was just wondering if Saul Bellow had arrived 30 years later in Chicago and got television first he might now be running his own corporation and none of this would ever have happened. I don't have the panoptic ease that Saul Bellow has in looking at this because I feel I am terrifically distracted, and enervated and the effort of keeping up with one's education is much greater now.

Bellow: Well we're all distracted. I quite agree, that's probably the best word to accompany the moronic inferno.

Amis: You've also talked about suspense as being the condition of life now.

Ignatieff: Waiting for the next shoe to drop.

Amis: Waiting for the next piece of event glamour, as you call it. That's a distraction as well.

Bellow: Well now you see this business of distraction is really terribly important. Last week I read an account of a new Nielson survey of television watching —

Ignatieff: Viewing.

Bellow: Viewing. Did you see that in *The Times*? It was fascinating because among other things it said that kids no longer watched a programme through. They have the clicker in their hands and they were channel hopping and so they were interested only in fragments of programmes. And their chief interest was in the special effects. They didn't care about the story. They didn't care about the characters. They were interested in the special effects, especially the noise effects. And this means that all coherence has gone. And this is sort of systematic destruction of coherence.

Amis: Of the narrative itself.

Bellow: That's right. Nothing is consecutive, everything is inconsequent, everything jumps out from strange corners. And really what this may create in the child or the adult too, is a sense of overwhelming sovereignty. 'I am the person whom all this serves and I am the one who makes all these decisions.'

Ignatieff: Because I have the button.

Bellow: Because I have the button and I'm immune to everything they can throw at me. I'm immune to a story.

Amis: You can't grip me.

Bellow: You can't grip me. You know, the Everyman, the old Everyman edition used to have a sort of a thing on the frontispiece saying 'a tale to hold old men from the chimney corner and children from their play.' Well that's not what holds them any more. What holds them is the scrambler, what holds them is scrambling.

Ignatieff: Yes.

Amis: And this of course will be market research, which is another great moronic instrument, I think. Is everyone in America a market researcher now? It sometimes seems that way. But they will look at this survey and they won't worry about the loss of the narrative line in human life, they will produce 10 minute programmes full of special effects geared to the short attention span.

Bellow: That's right, they go for the market directly.

Ignatieff: But this raises an interesting issue which I think we can move into another frame with, which is that if you've got everybody with the attention span of a flea, everybody increasingly kind of estranged from the magic of the story, the continuous attention and absorption of a story, it seems to me in some way this implies a

different kind of self, a different kind of individual watching. And I
know that's a tremendous concern of both of your writings, but I'm
wondering whether you could talk about this modern self. I mean, it
seems to me to be a self that has appetites but no centre. Desire but
no inner rule. I'm just wondering how that strikes you as a novelist.

Bellow: Well the ideal modern self seems to me to be a
fabrication. That is to say it does not emanate from deeper human
sources, it is made up in order to satisfy certain requirements of
personal advancement and of safety. And America's always been
that way in a sense. That is to say, from the beginning America has
received advice, Americans have received advice on what to be like
and how to behave.

Ignatieff: But the consequence is a self bombarded with advice
about how it should present itself but no inner —

Bellow: Well the true identity suffers erosion through this. And
disillusion. And I think that Europeans know very well what I'm
talking about because the same thing happened all over Europe. If
there hadn't been these erosions of identity, Hitler could not have
become what he became.

Ignatieff: (to Amis) You've called the character in your last novel
John Self. You must have had a reason. Doesn't this connect here?

Amis: Yes. He was to be a representative of appetite. If you listen
to your background radiation, your ordinary thoughts throughout a
day, it's a pretty sorry mess isn't it, even at the best of times? There
are little snarls and whimpers all through the day. And what the self
— we talk blithely of the self that is solid — what the solid self is
trying to do is to make that a kind of a narrative with some sort of
shape to it. My character, John Self, is abjectly a sort of 'no
comment' product of his time and therefore his head is full of the
distractions that are levelled at him. And thus, you know, much
degraded and much weakened.

Ignatieff: (to Bellow) But I want to go at it another way. One of
the things you said in an essay written in 1967, was 'we long for
enchantment but we're too sceptical.' I'm just wondering what you
meant then and what you meant by enchantment, because it could
mean political enchantment, it could mean sexual enchantment, it
could mean the enchantment of a story. It could mean something
very grand indeed.

Bellow: Well I'll tell you. Literature has always referred to a
world beyond the threshold of the world that we know and see. I
wouldn't want to say that it always had a religious foundation, it
didn't always. Well of course Christianity was a great power in this
respect. But the more what we called enlightenment spreads, the
more the disenchantment increases. So that, you know,
Shakespeare is a thoroughly enlightened genius; he is himself

sceptical about all these things, but of course he's always referring as a poet to the gods and the heavens and all the rest of that. Well that shrinks down in modern times. That becomes forbidden territory more and more, until we find ourselves standing on a thoroughly shrunken ground. Now what does one do about that? Does one say all of that was myth and religion and of no importance to us now, we've got to find something else? Or does one say this is a different kind of delusion —

Ignatieff: As Freud said.

Bellow: — another delusion? And I can no more credit that one than I can credit the supernatural. So what I do, and I'm sure Martin Amis is in the same situation, is to have some respect for his own intuitions and his deepest personal feelings as a creature who appears, he doesn't know how, on the face of the earth. Just like me, just like you. Doesn't know how he has come to be a human being, doesn't know how others have come to be what they are. That's really very mysterious. In other words, what I'm saying really is that the transcendent has been kicked out of modern literature on all sorts of grounds and I think we presume too much when we do that, you know. It's not right. And we're not being faithful to our own intuitions when we take it upon ourselves to say 'it's finished.' It's only finished in textbooks.

Amis: You're a splendid anachronism in this way. I mean, Saul Bellow writes in a style that — the high style, which has, as you say, been kicked upstairs, as it were, in modern literature. In the textbooks it's all pretty plain that literature used to be about gods, then it was about kings, then it was about heroes, then it was about you and me. And now it's about them. Even, you know, we live in the ironic age, even rock bottom realism is considered impossibly exotic and grand for the 20th century. It just seems to have gone that way.

Bellow: I think that's a very apt description of how it happened.

Ignatieff: (to Bellow) I wanted to get some personal experience into this because it just does seem to me that one of the things about your characters, if you'll allow me to go back to your books for a minute, but I'm interested in your own experience of this, is the deep embarrassment in the modern world of talking about metaphysics. That is, talking about the transcendent dimension. I mean, your characters not only run into trouble when they talk, when they want to be King Lear in the courtroom, they run into trouble when they want to talk about transcendence, the gods, what we would call the religious dimension. It's one of the great embarrassments of modern life, that you can't talk about this stuff without sounding like a lunatic.

Bellow: As long as that's a separate category of discourse, there's no point in talking about it. The words for it were used up a long time ago. So the only foundation for it is in actual experience, in one's own felt life. And if that isn't there, then there is really no point in sounding off about it in an abstract sense. That's exactly the difference between literature and other kinds of discourse. And that's why it's very hard for me to read books in which there's no personal sense of what really happens within the human being, but everybody is examining the rules from a logical standpoint or from a linguistic standpoint or so on, and it's all gobbledygook to me.

Ignatieff: So in a sense what you're saying there is that you're one of those people who hasn't succumbed to the embarrassment of talking about the transcendent, about this missing dimension, simply because it's something that you live as a human being and feel it.

Bellow: Well I don't know what Martin's experience was. I'll tell you something about my own. I went along always, I felt that intellectuals knew what they were talking about.

Ignatieff: Big mistake.

Bellow: It took me a long time to find out that some small number of them did know what they were talking about and most of them were terribly misleading. But in the meantime, to give you a short account of my mental life, I had gone through behaviourism and I'd gone through Marxism and I'd gone through psychoanalysis and I'd gone through existentialism and I'd gone through structuralism, and all of them evaporated. So I felt that I'd wasted my time, and the only profit I derived from it was to say 'no' to all of this and never to do it again, for anybody else.

Amis: You're saying too, aren't you, that why should a concern about what it is to be a human being be considered transcendental? I mean, the ground must have sunk very low if that scene is very high. It is *the* concern. It is what all writers should be addressing. And in fact one looks, sounds, feels like a crank the minute you bring it up.

Ignatieff: I'm just wondering, since Saul Bellow's given us a kind of short, personal biography of a history of disillusion, in a sense, whether you could do the same, Martin. I mean, how you've been led to the way you feel about the writer's essential business.

Amis: Well I'm happy to take Saul's word for it that most of the intellectuals don't know what they're talking about, because then I won't have to read them and can watch television instead. But my interests have always been strictly literary until quite recently. And now I'm realising that there is this subject called, I believe, non-fiction, that is full of interesting stuff. The study of man, in a sense. But I don't think disillusion quite describes what I feel. I feel that I'm in the middle of something and cannot yet see what it is. I think we all feel this a bit, that we don't know where we are until we're beyond it, and I'm not beyond it yet.

Bellow: Well I agree, I fully agree with Martin, and I apologise for the use of the word transcendent. I only wanted the audience to understand what I was talking about, and that's a handy word. But he's quite right. That is to say, that transcendence — transcendent is just a handle. It's not the real thing. The real thing is an unquenchable need that never stops gnawing at you. And you feel that, excuse me for using the word, you feel that you're being transcendent in that lousy sense when you are fully expressive. That's when it happens to you. Then you're satisfied that you've done the right thing. Otherwise no. Otherwise you do fall back on explanations and definitions and boring discourse, and, you know, you might as well be a social scientist and write that sort of thing.

Amis: That's the passionate element in — the passionate affluence?

Bellow: Right.

Amis: Yes.

Ignatieff: I'm just wondering, in this area, very difficult area of discussion, one of the things you said a long time ago which has stuck in my mind for a long time is the phrase 'ignorance of death is destroying us.'

Bellow: Well if you don't observe the power that death has, the unconscious power over the way people manage their lives, then you're not seeing what's happening at all. Because, well, take something like modern erotic life. If you omit the death factor from it, you don't know what's going on, you can't see it. But, you know, if you are a perishable subject and it's going to be all over within a certain time and you glory in your vigour and you want to collect as much sensual pleasure as you can, then you proceed with a certain urgency which only death can explain.

Ignatieff: Martin, I know that phrase 'ignorance of death is destroying us,' is one of the phrases that's important to you in Bellow's work. I'm just wondering why, why it's stuck with you, why you hold onto it.

Amis: Well, he says elsewhere that death is the dark backing a mirror needs before it can give off a reflection, that everything has to be seen in the context of death. Death has been made available to us more generously in this era than ever before. I wonder, do you mean it as part of one's own journey through life, that death is always there as the dark backing, or that it's the sinister black vein in life?

Bellow: Well I don't think that it's sinister, I think it's a natural thing and I think what they used to call the *timor mortis*, the fear of death, is also very natural. What's unnatural is to blank it out altogether and to dismiss it from your life in the gay whirl. That's where the mistake is made, it seems to me.

Amis: And just as we don't think about personal death, we don't think about global death too.

Bellow: Well, the plethora of events has forced a kind of indifference on us in this respect, you know. First there was the Great War, and then there was the Second World War, and then there was the Holocaust and then there was Gulag and there was the Great Terror of Stalin, and then there are the disasters which make such a din every day and assail us from all sides. And what are we supposed to feel about the earthquake in Mexico? What are we supposed to feel about the famine in Ethiopia? And since we are in the present age remarkably shallow in that respect anyhow, the thing to do is just to turn away from it and treat it as though it were something utterly unreal. Those are just dolls and dummies lying there.

Amis: While I was preparing that collection of essays *The Moronic Inferno*, I wondered what is it about this phrase that cut through me? And it was in August of this year, the time of the Hiroshima remembrances, and the moronic inferno as a phrase is a metaphor, in a sense. There isn't a moronic inferno, quite. It's not on fire. But there is a possible future in which the moronic inferno ceases to be a metaphor and is the description of the only available reality. And I'm sure when I got interested in this I thought I'd been writing about it all along, this thinned and violent life, as it seems to me now.

Bellow: None of this would matter if there were no such thing as human nature. That is to say, if there were not some unexplained inner primordial disagreement with what is happening. And I think that's what we have to refer ourselves to, otherwise what we're talking about is nonsense.

Ignatieff: Yes. And the disagreement, the inner primordial disagreement manifests itself above all, it seems to me, in a kind of loneliness. The deep, gnawing loneliness of a very gregarious, very busy, very active kind of social life. That is, the loneliness implicit in a lot of modern sexuality seems to me to be very poignant and also very terrible and a sign of that kind of inner refusal somehow.

Amis: Well, I think writers are very bad people to be consulted on solitude, because they have to be very keen on it.

Ignatieff: But don't you feel it? Don't you feel it in the culture? A kind of loneliness in the culture?

Amis: Well, it's a loneliness that occasionally forms into mobs is more how I feel it.

Bellow: Yes, that's what I meant when I said that the more the inner life is discredited, the more the public life grows in strength and this is what happens when you're in front of the — I go back again to our *bête noir*, the TV. That is to say, it's because of this impoverishment within that people turn outward. And they embrace events somehow, because in embracing these events they have at least a life which is collective and this is what everybody else is doing and everybody else is doing it from the same impulse. That is to say, because of this impoverishment. This is not a rejection of public life in the Aristotelian sense, this is just a description of the way it is now, and I hope that Aristotle would agree with me. I'm not about to twist his arm.

Ignatieff: I think we're moving to a close here and the question that I wanted to focus on is really this, how it is that a writer remains engaged with this question of what is going on out there in a world which is, in lots of ways that we've described tonight, very repellant and very frightening. I mean, the reflex of a kind of hatred for it is very easy, and it seems to me a reflex that you've both resisted very admirably and I'm just wondering how you sustain that engagement to search for that question, why you care about it?

Bellow: I don't know why I care about it, that's one of these questions that lead you to, into theology. But I do. And what a writer like me is apt to feel is that in all this moronic inferno, to go back to that again, there is some loss of the power to experience life. That people are really in a sense deprived of it now, to experience it in their own terms. And this has always been a sort of central impulse with American writers, and this is what Walt Whitman was all about. He said, you know, the idea is to be able to interpret what happens to you independently. And now it's all jargon, it's all nonsense, it's all slogans. It's all false descriptions and it's all fabrication. And of course, one resists that.

Amis: I think also that you're disqualified from real pessimism by being a writer. I think even the blackest writers, the Celines, even more a genuine hater of the modern world, still loves it because it is interesting. What it doesn't lose is interest. It may lose everything else but it still has that.

Ignatieff: I think that's where we should end. One of the great American critics, Alfred Kazin, once said that the real danger about facing modernity was the danger of easy hatred, easy contempt, easy fear for the violence and strangeness of modern life. It seems to me both Saul Bellow and Martin Amis are exemplary examples of novelists who've refused the temptation of easy hatred and continued to struggle with the question 'what is going on?'

CHAPTER 2

The Tough and the Tender

Michael Ignatieff,
with Ernest Gellner and Charles Taylor

Ignatieff: At the turn of the century William James said that at its core the debate about modernity is between the tough and the tender-minded. For the tough, the destruction of old traditions creates new freedoms, new knowledge, new opportunities. For the tender, the costs of all this destruction are simply too high: progress is purchased at the price of justice, belonging and community. For the tough, we simply have to grin and bear such costs of change; while for the tender, we have to get a grip on the growth machine before it tears up everything we value — nature, community, family — by the roots. Two leading figures in this debate about modernity and its costs are with me tonight: Ernest Gellner, Professor of Social Anthropology at Cambridge and author of a dozen books on social thought, a consistent critic of nostalgia and sentimentality as responses to modernity, and Charles Taylor, a philosopher and political theorist at Oxford and McGill, who has consistently championed the tender-hearted critique of modernity against its tough-minded adversaries. I'm just wondering whether we could begin by having you define what you mean by modernity. And then to get you to focus clearly on where your disagreements then follow. And I thought I'd begin with you, Charles Taylor.

Taylor: As you just put it, and maybe Ernest agrees with you, it sounds as though modernity is mainly defined by a series of instruments we now have at our disposal, like bureaucracy, the market and so on, which are purely sort of neutral instruments and have a big pay off but have a high psychic cost. I think modernity has to be defined, anyway in our civilisation, in a quite different way. There are certain — and here this is a Weberian train of thought — there are certain very important, you might say almost spiritual, goals or ideals or values which arose in the West. And I'll just name two which I think power and are behind this modern society: a certain modern idea of freedom, well several, a family of ideas, we'll go into that and fight about that I'm sure later; and secondly, the notion that the centre of life, of the purpose of life, of the meaning of life, is to be found in what I want to call 'ordinary life' itself, that is the life of the family, the life of production, as against most previous civilisations which have had a notion that there is something beyond ordinary life, some higher type of activity or perhaps otherworldly type of worship or something of that kind which is the centre of human life, what human life is all about. This modern culture stresses the intrinsic value of the life of production and reproduction. I think these are the two things that power modern civilisation. And we shouldn't just look at modernity as a lot of these instruments came along here, you know, bureaucracy or the market or the break-up of earlier communities, and they turn out to be very useful and we kind of went along with them because they raised GNP. It's as though they didn't have any more powerful draw on us than their purely utilitarian ones. And I think that we get entirely off on the wrong track if we define it that way. Because in fact the malaise of modernity is not just because we paid a price for these instruments, but because we're also hooked on the intrinsic values that go along with these instruments and we have to work out those values and we find it almost impossible to do so.

Gellner: Instead of beginning, as you do, Charles, with values and ideas — I'd like to get to those later — I'd like to begin with very straightforward general features of modern society, of the kind of society which has already emerged in the successfully developed countries and which is emerging in the rest. Now, the first thing about it, it's totally unique. It's a society totally different from any other society which has ever existed before, and its distinguishing features are worth listing. They're terribly obvious. One, it's the first society ever to be based on cognitive growth. It doesn't assume individual discoveries, it assumes that there's a kind of perpetual series of discoveries to be made, that the cognitive capital of mankind is growing, is growing in principle, that we've cracked the problem of making it grow. We're not to speak despairingly asking 'how are we going to find about what the world is like?', we know that we can find out. I mean, the justified cognitive optimism is unique. It's a society based on knowledge. And this has enormous implications. And I think when we start debating those implications you and I will disagree very profoundly. What goes with this is that the cognitive growth has practical applications, I mean, obviously through technology affluence. This is the first real affluent society. As you know, the theory that pre-agrarian society was affluent, in a sense, and if that theory is correct and it's disputed in anthropology, it was only affluent in the sense that people's needs were small, consequently they were fairly easily satisfied. But our society's affluent in the strong sense that without necessarily limiting needs. In fact one of the accusations notoriously made against our society is that it artificially augments needs, even when it does so it is capable of satisfying them. We're no longer living in a Malthusian world. Our entire politics is determined by — the main method of social control is generalised bribery. So you buy off discontent. And the society is in trouble when occasionally this cornucopia gets jammed and the stuff stops coming out, as it has since the early seventies, the society's in trouble because it's normally used to buying off discontent.

Ignatieff: (to Taylor) I sense you chafing under this diagnosis.

Taylor: Oh definitely, definitely. I mean, it gets worse — on each of those progressive three points. But on the cognitive growth point, I mean of course it's right in one very important sense, that this is the first society based on the endless growth of science and technology. But right there is hidden tremendous self-misunderstanding, in that we tend to think that the same is true for growth in knowledge about ourselves as we know to be true in growth of knowledge about the natural universe surrounding us. We therefore have a way of reinterpreting all our problems as technological problems, as problems to be solved. Even the word problem-solve, of course is sort of redolent with that outlook, and then we completely fail to understand ourselves and what we really face, the difficulties we really face and dilemmas we really face. That's why I started right off saying it's a question of our spiritual outlook and these difficulties are not difficulties that can be just overcome by problem-solving. And I want to point out right away that that's part of the culture itself: that we tend to see our problems as problems in those terms. Because you see, I mean, the reason, in principle, to put it in a nutshell, maybe we should talk about this, why that kind of scientific method which is so obviously successful in natural science can't have that pay off about ourselves, is that we're self-interpreting beings. We are partly constituted by the way we understand ourselves. And we grow and change by re-interpreting and re-understanding ourselves in different ways. The more we think that we're simply other objects of natural science to be, as it were, empirically examined, and there are certain facets of us of course which are like that, but the more we think that our central questions of our identity and what we're about and so on can be understood in that way, the more we're barking up the wrong tree, looking in the wrong direction, and discussing central issues in a completely inapt language. In a language that will never somehow get to the issue. And actually this myth of modern science as applied to ourselves actually impedes understanding, actually impedes enlightening debate, actually impedes insight.

Gellner: But I'm not sure we ought to be distracted —

Taylor: I'm not attacking your science, because your science doesn't actually proceed that way.

Gellner: Oh I'm not personally touchy. I mean, you can attack that. I'm inclined to think any science in which I'm a professor must be phoney. Which takes care of three sciences, you know. But I would like to come back to this business of the self. And if I may, sum up the way I think he sees it. And I think this is absolutely fundamental. I think he's put it roughly in these terms in various books. There are two kinds of self. There's the pre-modern self, which is part of the cosmos, where the environment, social and natural, of which it's a part, makes a kind of meaningful whole which is described and articulated in the same terms as he described himself, so this life is part of the kind of continuum, as the saying goes 'life makes sense, life is meaningful.' And then there is the modern self, which is not part of the cosmos but what you call nature. Where the nature's an impersonal orderly system in no way designed on the same principles as himself, in no way underwriting his aims and his values. And his attitude toward this is a kind of, you know, he's Robinson Crusoe thrown into it. Manipulative, indifferent, nature's not supportive. And the difference, I think, in in our attitudes is not that we disagree in this diagnosis, I think this is a pretty accurate account of what has happened, but I think that this modern, rather lonely, not underwritten, unlegitimated, isolated self, is an inescapable price of the cognitive advances by which we live.

Ignatieff: Okay, that is where the issue then gets very clearly focused.

Gellner: This is the real issue. We agree on the diagnosis. This is what the change has been. From a kind of man who is mating with the world to the man who is not mating with the world. But I think it's inevitable and we shouldn't cheat about it. And the disagreement is Charles is much too sympathetic to the fashionable philosophies which try to inject a lot of saccharine into the situation, and sort of sugar-coat it.

Taylor: I think, okay, it's a clear disagreement. So, maybe we should focus on sort of the green outlook, you might call it. I mean, people who are in ecological movements and have some sense which they would articulate maybe this way, that we after all belong to some larger order, the universe is not just there to be used by us as a kind of trash can. We have an obligation to something bigger than ourselves. Now, these people, they sound pre-modern in a way because they are striking this chord of 'we belong to a larger cosmic order' which sounds like pre-16th century, and your reaction to that would be 'I'm sorry boys and girls, this faded out three centuries ago. We've lost that. Stop looking backward.' And while I agree with you that we can't look backward to exactly those cosmological views, I think there's a very profound truth underlying that, and that hunger is not all wrong. That is, that there is a sense in which we are part of a larger order, that in order to understand ourselves we have to see ourselves as part of a larger order of nature, and that part of what we're striving for, even as modernists, to understand ourselves expressively, to come to terms with and understand ourselves expressively requires that we acknowledge that. And that a definition of ourselves purely as, if you like, punctual selves in a world surrounded with instrumental objects fails to understand the forces within us. I mean, the challenge to any understanding of the self, the real challenge for us to meet, is it has to explain why we're committed to, we're strongly moved by, the values and goals that we are. And can that view of the self really give an account of why we are so passionate about our understanding of freedom, even the understanding of freedom that's linked with it, why it's a passionate moral goal, understanding of fulfilment, our yearning for some kind of unity with nature? And I think, that test it just totally flunks. And that's why that view has to be somehow amended.

Gellner: Well, this is absolutely the heart of the matter, and I'd like to make a correction, confession, and then a counter-attack. Now the correction is you've said that 'this is the view of the self that you like'. Well, I don't like it. I don't terribly enjoy it, I just think, in honesty, it's a price to be paid. It's not something I like, I just don't wish to avoid and evade it. So don't tell me I like it, I don't. That's the correction. A confession is your main charge is you can't explain your own commitment to freedom, to intellectual honesty, which in fact is a kind of paradoxical self-contradiction, because I insist on this vision, in the name of honesty, in the sense of not deceiving ourselves, you say 'well there you are, you make a big fuss about intellectual honesty, where the devil do you get that from?' But anyway, my main confession is 'yes, I cannot, but I've got to live with this.' This is my main position. And then the counter-charge is that you're having it both ways. I mean, you say 'well it isn't the kind of justification which used to exist in the days of Plato.' I mean, I think Plato is right to be taken as a paradigm of the kind of legitimations which prevailed when our legitimation crisis, which is supposed to be our topic, didn't exist. There was another one but not ours, where a hierarchically organised cosmos legitimated what Plato considered the best strivings within a soul. The stratification of a soul, the stratification of society, the stratification of pleasures and satisfactions, the stratification of kinds of knowledge, the stratification of kinds of objects in the world. There were kind of five types of stratification all dovetailing and reinforcing each other so you could ultimately answer the puzzle question of 'why be just?' with saying 'well, you're really truly being yourself and the whole world is so organised that sound values are underwritten.' And this style of legitimation prevailed until modernity came along. The nature of the world underwrote what people considered their best values. My point is first of all they were cheating. The arguments were blatantly circular. Secondly, it's not compatible with genuine knowledge. Now, genuine knowledge is a style of cognitive exploration codified in the 18th century and on the whole agreed in outline, which means that you don't know what's going to turn up. Genuine knowledge is a hypothetical deductive. You have an idea but the intrinsic, inherent pleasingness or fittingness of the idea is no warranty of its truth. The only way of validating is actually finding out whether the world is like that. And you can't tell in advance. Consequently you cannot link your social order to genuine cognitive beliefs because the cognitives are up for grabs. You never know what's going to turn up tomorrow. And as you want society to be reasonably stable, the two have got to be separated. You've got to have a separation of cosmology and practical politics. And that kind of old legitimation doesn't work. You are kind of having it both ways. Saying, well it's not just like that. I mean, you're with me that far. Nevertheless, in order to explain our best strivings, we must make attributions about ourself. Well, is this knowledge or isn't it? It's a kind of half-way world which tries to have it both ways. And this is why I don't go with you. You obfuscate the issue in certain things.

Taylor: Let's focus on the weakness of your position before we look at the weakness of my position.

Gellner: Oh, I'd like it the other way round.

Taylor: I think that your argument here is just an absolute paradigm case of what I was saying earlier about the way in which a certain cognitive model has obfuscated the issue. And instead of asking ourselves where do we best get knowledge and understanding, we come at it with a model of how knowledge and understanding ought to work which we sort of impose on reality. Now, hypothetical deductive is just nothing to the purpose here. In the field of self-understanding, the name of the game, if you like, is to try to give an interpretation which makes sense of what cannot be denied in one's own being, in what one is about. To explain it. And you've just admitted, in a sense, that the theory you're proposing doesn't do that. Well then, let's apply this kind of Popperian model in a general way, in this quite different intellectual fashion. Instead of a Popperian model of falsification of hypotheses, let's have a Popperian model of the scrapping of self-understandings that manifestly don't actually meet their goal, right? That would mean that you'd have to introduce a richer notion of the self to make sense of yourself. I mean, something like — we have to understand human beings as beings that have something we can call an identity. They have a notion of who they are, which is central to not only their self-understanding but even to their operating as moral agents. And if we explore the conditions of that, as we are today, then we get back again to some conception of history, sometimes of community, which is how people identify themselves, of continuity, and we get back again to certain political conditions that we have to meet in order to go on being the kind of beings that we are.

Gellner: I very much suspect you can't have it both ways. You want to make half of the old goodies and some of the modern egalitarianism into a kind of blend, and I don't think that particular cocktail will work. I think your initial charge was you just have a kind of *a priori* model of what knowledge is like, the kind of thing that you like doesn't fit into it, and so it's arbitrarily excluded. No, I think there are very good reasons — it's not arbitrary that I happen to take out a certain kind of model of knowledge and then exclude what you want because it doesn't fit. I have a certain model of knowledge, and for good reasons which can be expounded, this is it. This has given the technological power which we have, which has enabled us first of all to be egalitarian, which you like. Secondly, it has enabled us to take some of the sting out of political conflict. Don't live on it and then spit on it. You can't — that's part of my case against you.

Ignatieff: All right, can I break in here and try and summarise at least where we've got to? We have in these disagreements, I think, two competing conceptions of the self at issue. And it seems to me that it could be said that you're simply reconciled to certain kinds of alienation. You spoke of the alienation involved in knowledge itself. You spoke of the alienation involved in a self that can no longer ground itself in a cosmic order.

Gellner: That's dead right.

Ignatieff: Then, it seems to me, we have to focus on the question of what costs of modernity are just too high. What I hear you saying is 'look, you can't have it both ways. If you want modernity's gains you've got to live with its costs.' Well then it seems to me the following issue is focused: which costs are just too high? I'm not clear that any costs are too high for you. When you, for instance, discuss people's discontent with modernity as a *maladie imaginaire*, as an imaginary disease, I get the feeling that you're pretty well prepared to buy the whole package. That's my problem with your position. (to Taylor) My problem with your position is I can't figure out which costs you're actually prepared to bear. Could we focus on that issue, because I think that would take us further.

Gellner: Well, my accusation against Charles is that he won't face it as squarely as you've put it to him. It's not that he won't pay some of the costs, he will paper over it, he will say 'well actually we can have it both ways. We don't have to go back to hierarchical platonic worlds in which the self is underwritten by cosmic order, but we can still have a self which is a damn sight better than a kind of thrown into the world solitary atom, simply using the world as an alien object. We can have something better than that. And this something better, we can actually know about it.' And this is the point, of course, of my major charge. You ask, what kind of price are we prepared to pay? Well, I'm saying we've already paid it. We can't go back. The price has been paid. What we can do is sugarcoat it, paper it over, and which I temperamentally dislike doing, thereby exemplifying the commitment to those values which then Charles uses against me to say, 'well yes, I have those values but I don't underwrite them. I just have them.'

Ignatieff: (to Taylor) So are you having it both ways?

Taylor: No, I'd see the thing totally differently from Ernest, because — well let's put it this way: I agree that there are big dilemmas in modern society, which if you describe them in a very general and vague way we can call the same dilemmas. For instance, the dilemma between belonging to a community and realising oneself, fulfilling oneself as a free individual. I think this comes out in all sorts of ways and you see it in the whole strain on the family today, you see it in the strain between community and individual. In some very general sense that is a huge constituent of dilemma that modern people live through, right? Now, the issue between us is how we, in a more fine-grained way, understand that, which we have to do if we're going to come to grips with it as individuals or as societies. And I think that Ernest's way of coming to grips with it is just very very wrong. It's not that I want to have it both ways in the sense that I have an easy solution to this dilemma. I don't think it is easily soluble, and in one sense I probably agree with you in this way, that it'll be with us till the end of time or we blow ourselves up or something of that kind. But I really think that the way of understanding it which you have is very, very wrong-headed, because it doesn't really understand the forces on both sides of this dilemma. The forces pulling us towards individualism and the forces that pull us towards some kind of community. And it doesn't understand that, and I return to my charge because this picture of the self that you think we have to settle for is just wrong.

Gellner: Now take the other element in your romantic pro-expressivist desire for a notion of the self which is more at peace with the community: the only way to do it in the large anonymous mass society is by major productions, political theatrical productions, such as are in effect typical of the authoritarian regimes of the thirties. I mean, they seized upon this point, that people want politics to be politics of the theatre, where belongingness, to some extent hierarchy, but certainly belongingness — incidentally, exclusion of the outsider and so on — were all deeply

symbolised so that their affective life and their political life
dovetailed precisely in the kind of way which you seem to desire.
Now, the opposition, alas, gives encouragement to that. The
romantic Left and the romantic Right do sometimes meet. But —
let me just finish the point — you said that liberal democracy
expresses our, presumably Western European, deepest impulses.
It's not obvious to me, alas.

Taylor: I would maintain that because of what we are and the
requirement of living in citizen democracies that we, I think, have,
we need some on-going sense of community identification. And I
could go into the reasons for that step in the argument, but I think
that they're an essential underpinning to citizen participation.
Without some kind of what Montesquieu called 'virtue', some kind
of sense of common purposes, among anyway a large percentage of
the population, citizen democracy just tends to break down. So my
way of putting the issue is: we need some kind of citizen
identification. Now there are all sorts of very nasty and extremely
horrifying ways this can be produced, including ways that actually
negate participatory freedom by their very nature, like what you
mentioned, fascism and nazism and certain kinds of nationalism
today, and we could mention lots of other cases, but that our choice,
our genuine choice, is not between all of these on the one hand and
then total absence of any identification on the other, but between
the good, healthy kinds, I mean the kinds that we can live with and
kinds that we can't live with.

Ignatieff: But how can we guarantee the good, healthy kinds?

Taylor: You don't guarantee the good, healthy kinds, the best
way to get the bad kind is to try not to have any at all, and then you
let the —

Gellner: The way they justified themselves, the expressivist
excessive Right-wing regimes really justify themselves precisely by
saying 'at last the outer and the inner are in congruence. The outer
ritual, the outer participation and the inner feeling are in harmony
at last.' And they had a point. It wasn't entirely false. And the main
nazi critique of Weimar was that the outward institutions and the
inner feelings didn't cohere. They used language which overlaps
with yours: that the purely instrumental, technical outer world
didn't correspond to the deep inner feelings. And the justification
of this new romanticism was precisely to broaden the congruence.
Well you can't have it both ways. If this is what you want, if your
complaint against excessive modernity is the insulation of the self,
I'm not quite clear in the name of what you reject some versions
which are very full-blooded and, alas, gave the participants an
enormous amount of satisfaction while pretending to reject them.

Taylor: We're still talking past each other. It's not that I'm sitting here in a disenchanted world and I have a complaint that it's not coloured enough.

Gellner: I thought that's precisely what the situation was.

Taylor: Oh no, no, no. My point is that that picture of us in a disenchanted world is in a very important way wrong. That we do live by very important values, we don't exist as disenchanted subjects. And my question is what do these values commit us to, or what are the preconditions of our being able to go on existing living by these values? When I ask that question I come up with — just to be short and quick, speak in slogans — the necessity for some kind of community identification. And then I see the issue as what kind? So it's not that I have this great hunger for some kind of belonging, give me any kind, whatever brand, quick. That's not the point. I think that without that our society breaks down, and I would say the fastest way to hand it over to the Ayatollah Khomeinis of this world or the Jerry Falwell, or name your particular brand or particular country, is to make a desert of public space by treating it simply, or thinking we can live treating it simply instrumentally. There is that requirement even to keep a democratic society going. That there be some kind of public identification. It's either going to come from a form of self-understanding which puts freedom and self-identification and participation at its centre, or it's going to come from some other forms, be they religious fundamentalist or whatever, or nationalist, of course, in the most common case that I've been grappling with in our country, Michael's and mine, in the last few years, a kind of blind nationalism. The only way to defeat this is not to pretend that it neither corresponds to a real need of individuals, nor corresponds to a real demand on society, that's the way just of giving over the victory. The only way to combat this is to understand what the forces are and try to give a better answer to them. You're not guaranteed success, but it's absurd to think that going to conjure this demon by — these demons aren't conjured by saying the devil doesn't exist, right? It's a conjuring trick you're doing.

Gellner: No, that's my charge against you.

Taylor: I see (laughs)

Ignatieff: Who's the conjurer here, the magician?

Gellner: I see myself as bravely looking at a bleak reality. I hope it's bravely. And trying to pour cold water on the attempts to elude it. The specific example you chose of the need for national belonging, I would accept. But I think the mechanisms of it are much more specific than you admit. I mean, you take this as a general example of the need of the self to be underwritten by the social and general environment. Now the particular force of modern nationalism seems to me to spring precisely from very specific circumstances of a mass, atomised, mobile society in which the sub-communities are eroded, in which people do not interact as other members of intimate communities, but interact with a large number of individuals who they've never seen before and they'll never see again. Where the communication has to be contextless — context-free — where the actual message has to communicate as opposed to the context. And where it has to be based on a sort of shared education-transmitted culture. I mean, we began by trying to give the general characteristics of modernity. I would say there's a third feature which I didn't get to, and that is that the modern world is the first one in which the high culture is not a specialty, not a privileged accomplishment of a small, clerical elite, but pervades the entire society. Not because we're so kind as to diffuse it and give it to the lower orders, because society can't work otherwise. Because the kind of jobs that are done nowadays all presuppose literacy and standardised script, and once this obtains of course people's major commitment is to the culture in which the economic unit operates. Because unless they're integrated and acceptable in that culture they are unemployable. So in that sense I agree with you. Nationalism is a great imperative. But I don't feel like saying whoopee about this. I don't know whether you are enthusiastic about it.

Ignatieff: I think this discussion has in a way caricatured your position into a kind of teeth-clenched stoical acceptance of the costs of modernity when I think in fact you're much more partisan of modernity. It's not simply a question of facing up to its costs but actually accepting and welcoming its advantages. Am I right in this?

Gellner: You're dead right. I mean, I don't mind this Walter Mitty fantasy of somebody stoically accepting the ardours of modernity, but in fact, as you say, I'm much warmer. I mean, there are two things to be said in favour of modernity. One, it's inevitable and second, it's good. And it's not good because it's inevitable, but it's good on top of being inevitable. But it is very important that it is inevitable. I mean, mankind first of all has now got hooked on a style of living to which he would like to get accustomed and simply will not, freely, without the most appalling political disasters, accept some kind of reverse policy and a serious romantic rejection of the modern world. You know, that particular programme is just unthinkable, incidentally would involve the elimination of vast numbers of people who simply wouldn't then be able to survive. So it's simply not a remotely realistic alternative. But on top of that, I mean it seems to me positively good that we should have overcome scarcity, that economic and political conflicts in society should have ceased to be a zero sum game, that it would be possible to avoid unnecessary physical suffering. I think on all that we can agree.

After that it's partly a matter of stress, partly a matter of kind of philosophical aesthetics, partly a matter of strategy and tactics. Let's begin with the most trivial: the philosophical aesthetics, because it matters least, in a way. The disagreement is I don't like camouflaging the fact that we've paid a philosophical price for modernity. The affluent world lives by genuine knowledge. Genuine knowledge is incompatible with a kind of illusion of absolute legitimation which mankind previously lived by. We've got to do without it, full stop. There are more important political issues and strategic tactical questions hinging on where we go from there. One is I think there's a danger in wanting the re-enchantment. I mean, Charles has a book on Hegel where in fact it presents Hegel and Marxism, not as a fulfilment of the Enlightenment but as an overcoming of the weakness of the Enlightenment. Namely, the end of alienated and mechanical, atomised man. Now that desire and the encouragement of indulging in that desire does seem to me to lead to excesses both on Right and Left. On the Left it leads to the romantic theory that after scarcity it'll be possible also to do without government and coercion, which has of course had the disastrous consequence that one part of the developed industrial world has no language in which to talk about its own political problems because they're not supposed to exist in the first place, so they can't discuss them. It's not merely because it's repressed, they just don't have the language in which to do it. And this seems to me tragic. On the Right, of course, it leads to kind of romantic expressivist politics which you both dislike, but I don't quite see how you can avoid. Now, it seems to me the correct way to go on from there is to study the mechanics — you don't like the word because it implies a kind of mechanistic attitude to society — which will enable us to face the various problems of affluent industrial society, a society which has overcome scarcity, where productive resources grow faster than population. In fact a non-Malthusian society, a non-zero sum game society. And those problems are various. One of them is how to stop destroying the environment? How does it shift from its ingrained obsession with material goods, which are now used in the more affluent section of the population simply as symbols for status? How do you persuade them to have some other status symbols, like the Galbraith-Hersch problem? And the other problem, which I think is the main one, what are the rules of politics? What are the structural constraints, talking in a pompous sociological way, what are the ways of preserving liberty? Don't ask for me to justify my commitment to liberty, you just have to take that as a datum. But it does seem to me enormously precarious. On the way to industrial, scientific affluent society we had liberty but the two were intimately linked. The precise details are very much under dispute. But there's no doubt about it. The one thing favoured the other, and one thing was a precondition of the other, and we got the two together. I'm not at all convinced that there aren't very major forces at work in developed societies which militate against liberty. And our main task, of course, is to find out what those contraints are and do something about it, as far as possible at least. Our job is to understand the world not to change it. I don't have any presumptions about trying to change it, but if I can make a contribution to understanding it I'll be well content. Now the pursuit of new major legitimations seems to me an obstacle in this task. I would like to see us concentrate on what are the mechanics which lead us away from a liberal society. And I think the forces are very considerable. And of course the late industrialisers may not have had the liberalism to begin with. This is a further problem. What are the preconditions of preservation or extension of liberty, rather than, I think, a wild goose chase after recovery of an old central identity with the world, the old kind of self? That's the state of the debate as I see it.

Ignatieff: How do you see it, Charles?

Taylor: Totally different. You see I think we really are speaking from completely incommensurable views of this because —

Gellner: I thought not.

Taylor: Well, paradoxically I come out from my point of view as more gung-ho, more affirmative of modernity than Ernest.

Gellner: Strange.

Taylor: Strange. Because I'm supposed to be cast in the other role here in Ernest's scenario. But the thing is that I not only think it's a wonderful thing that we have greater longevity and greater numbers of people who can live above the poverty line and all these things that we have that we didn't have in any other period of human history, I also think that there is something great and magnificent and even exhilarating in our modern understanding of freedom. Modernity has opened new spiritual horizons to mankind. So, far from the clenched teeth version of things, I think there's something great in this. The way I see the problem is that we have a certain set of dangers, even of self-destruction and self-stultification in modernity which centre around — let me pick out just the particular ones that worry me — centre around the self-destruction of citizen participatory societies, which I think are at the heart even of our conflict about the environment. And in order to come to grips with them we have to develop a better understanding of what our own actual spiritual sources are as moderns. And there I think we come to a point where my whole outlook, I admit, gets perhaps very hard to believe, because it has a certain twist to it which I will confess before you point it out to me. It's that there's some kind of inherent tendency in this modern development to misunderstand ourselves. The job of understanding just what we are committed to and what modern identity is about is a perpetually difficult one which involved criticising and peeling away illusions which are somehow more plausible first off, on the face of it. I think the mass of the important illusion which is more plausible on the face of it, from my point of view, is your position, this particular view about knowledge, the simple empiricist model of knowledge, the conception of the disengaged self, the conception of the purely disenchanted universe. I connect that conception of the self with part of the blindness which comes out in our political, as it were, self-destruction of our citizen life. And so I think that one does something important if one punctures that illusion and develops a richer and I think truer conception of the self. So I don't see myself as in the business of re-enchanting the universe. I see myself, on the contrary, as trying to get clearer, truer, get a more authentic self-knowledge of the actual values and goals that we all live by. And from that develop certain consequences about how we should structure our political life. And when you get there, then I think you see that, although I won't deny the importance of mechanisms and gimmicks in politics — I mean, who who's been in politics could? They play a role — they just aren't going to be enough to regenerate citizen democracy in our civilisation.

Ignatieff: Beneath what seems to me a kind of agreeable consensus between the two of you about the values of a liberal democratic society, I hear a fundamental disagreement about what politics can be about. I mean, when I listen to you, Ernest Gellner, I get the feeling by and large that you think the language of actually existing politics in the West, which is a language which is mostly about the preservation of liberty, somehow, is more or less adequate to our situation. That is to say the politics that ordinary people think is politics is actually addressing the real problems we face, which is how to keep the growth machine going, how to keep us free, how to keep us democratic. Whereas I think what I hear Charles Taylor saying is that there's a whole dimension of current human aspiration, there's a whole dimension of our problems even, the malaise of modernity which has simply dropped out of sight in our politics. That is, what we talk about politically, our language is somehow not adequate to our problems. I think there is a disagreement here about the adequacy of political language and also a disagreement about what politics is about.

Gellner: There's one strand in Charles' thinking and may be present in you as well, that effectiveness of the kind of liberal, pluralistic and haggling politics presupposes an undercurrent of agreement and values. And this may well be true. That, in other words, it's not a matter of institutions, it is a matter of a shared political culture, and unless you have it the other thing wouldn't work. This may well be true. I'm not necessarily disagreeing with it. Nor do I disagree with the other thing which you're hinting at, that there are other things than the maintenance of liberty and the production of goodies. I mean, the shift to a post-affluent society, to one which tries to de-fetishise material symbols and preserve the natural environment and so on. The one which has sound mechanisms for controlling that big slice of resources which it gives to the centre, and at the same time doesn't totally erode local community. I mean, I accept all that. I'm not in fact nearly as much in disagreement as you suggest.

Ignatieff: But don't you have, in a way, a self-denying ordinance in your view of the world, when you talk about 'let's not get into the business of re-legitimising the world, let's not get into the business of re-enchantment?' It's a self-denying ordinance about politics. It's saying politics is about the orderly management of the modern world. It's not about giving people a chance to fulfil themselves as citizens. And I just think that is a cleavage between the two of you.

Gellner: And it's a secularisation of what used to be called the 'end of ideology', the taking of absolutes out of politics, I don't mind that. I think a society which can get away with it is lucky.

Taylor: But no one gets away with it. You either do it unconsciously and dangerously and self-defeatingly and potentially disastrously or you do it hopefully, consciously and perhaps avoiding some of the worst consequences. We do it all the time. If you look at our modern politics, the politicians may be talking about dollars and cents or pounds and pence or goods or distribution or taxes and so on, but what's actually making the running is very often moral stances, moral images. Take these two, Thatcher and Reagan there, they are in a kind of way that I find sometimes horrifying, they are deeply moralising figures, projecting moral self-images, projecting poles of identification, alas, all too successfully in my view, in their respective societies. And that's what a lot of the politics is actually about. That's what's making it go. That's what's winning elections and why can't we talk about this as against pretending —

Ignatieff: But doesn't that point work against what you're arguing in a sense? That's moral politics with a vengeance. Doesn't that — Thatcher and Reagan — doesn't that precisely vindicate soulless pragmatism in politics? It is keeping morality out of politics as much as possible, because otherwise if you bring it in people just hit you over the head.

Taylor: That, to me, is equivalent to saying because of all the very unsuccessful and even horrifying forms of sexual life that may exist in human life let's do without sex. I mean the answer is, forget it, it's impossible. This is not what human life is all about, this is not where we're at. The only way to defeat this bad kind of stuff is by a good version of the same stuff. And you're just deluding yourself if you think that politics can fail to be about that. Because even when politics seems to be about pure matters of good distribution, that is even when the actual content of what they're saying on television to each other purely concerns the distribution of income and taxes and so on, a real look at what's going on in the political process tells you that what is appealing, swinging votes also of course touches on distribution of goods, but is also something else.

Ignatieff: Okay, I think this is the moment when I think we should try and draw the discussion together. It seems to me that this discussion has vindicated the idea that the really substantive disagreements between people are not adequately described by the slogans of Right and Left, Capitalist and Socialist — that undercutting these disagreements, beneath them, working through them, is a much more fundamental disagreement about modernity of the kind that we've had exposed here tonight, between those who welcome modernity, who believe its gains far outweigh its costs, who believe that the freedom that modernity has brought comes as a complete and novel human liberation. And those for whom the costs of modernity are troubling and unresolved and unconfronted by our politics. It's not necessarily a simple disagreement between those who are for modernity and those who are against modernity. And I think if you come out of listening to this discussion tonight with a sense that the politics you read in the newspapers and on the television just doesn't begin to touch the kinds of issues that have been raised here, this discussion will have been a very useful one.

CHAPTER 3

The Culture of Narcissism

Michael Ignatieff
with Christopher Lasch & Cornelius Castoriadis

Ignatieff: Perhaps the most painful cost of modernity is the loss of community and neighbourhood. In a world of strangers, we seem to withdraw more and more to the family and home, our haven from a heartless world. Yet our political traditions tell us that a sense of community is a human necessity, that we can only become full human beings when we belong to each other as citizens and neighbours. Without such a public life, our selves begin to shrink to a hollow private core. What is modernity doing to our identities? Are we becoming more selfish, less capable of political commitment, readier to pull up the drawbridge on our neighbours?

To explore these issues are Christopher Lasch, an American historian, author of *The Culture of Narcissism* and more recently *The Minimal Self* and the best-known critic of the void at the heart of the modern identity; and Cornelius Castoriadis, French psychoanalyst and social theorist, who has been at the forefront of French debates about the self and society for nearly 40 years. Cornelius Castoriadis, how would you describe the change in our public lives?

Castoriadis: Well, for me the problem arose for the first time at the end of the fifties, with what I was seeing already at the time as the crumbling of the working class movement, of the revolutionary project which had been linked with this movement. And I was, I think, forced to describe a change in capitalist society which was at the same time a change in the type of individuals which this society was more and more producing. The change in society I think we'll come to later. The change in individuals was the fact that, to put it very briefly, because of the bankruptcy of traditional working class organisations, trade unions, parties and so on, because of the disgust with what was happening, because also of the ability during this period of capitalism to grant a rising level of living and to enter the period of consumerism, people were turning their back, so to speak, on common interests, common activities, on public activities, were refusing to take responsibility, and were retrenching in a sort of — within quotation marks — 'private' world. That is, family and a very few relations. I say within quotation marks because we ought to avoid misunderstandings there.

Ignatieff: What misunderstandings, Cornelius?

Castoriadis: Philosophical distinctions. You see . . well, nothing is ever fully private. I mean, even when you dream, you have words, and these words you have borrowed from the English language. You see what I mean? And what we call individual is in a certain sense a social construct.

Ignatieff: Now, a sceptic would say that the critique of selfishness and individualism in capitalist society is just as old as capitalist society itself. It goes back 300 years. So what do you say to that sceptic? I mean, how do you convince them that the modern self, the modern post-war self of a consumer capitalist society is a different kind of self, that there's a new kind of individualism, a new kind of selfishness even?

Lasch: What we have is not so much old-fashioned self-aggrandisement and acquisitive individualism, which, as you say, has been subject to criticism from the moment this new kind of individualist personality came into being in the 17th-18th century. But this kind of individualism seems to have given way to the retrenchment that Cornelius spoke of a minute ago — it's a good way of gaining access on some of this, I think. I've talked of a minimal self, or of a narcissistic self, as a self that's increasingly emptied of any kind of content and which has to find the goals of life in the narrowest possible terms. I think, increasingly, in terms of raw survival, daily survival, as if daily life were so problematic, as if the world were so threatening and uncertain that the best you could hope to do was simply to get by. To live one day at a time. And indeed, this is the therapeutic advice, in the worst sense, that people are given in our world.

Ignatieff: But, survival, Christopher? Aren't you going a little far there? I mean, some people might not recognise that, they might think survival applies to the victims of some terrible tragedy or something, but you're talking about daily life in the richest society in the world. Why survival?

Lasch: That's one way of defining what's new, I think. While survival has always been a preoccupation, overriding preoccupation for people, for most people, it's only in our time that it seems to have acquired almost a kind of moral status. As if survival were not the precondition, material survival, to a moral life —

Ignatieff: But all there was.

Lasch: But all there was. If one were to go back to the Greeks, I think one could see very clearly the difference for the Greeks, for Aristotle in particular. The precondition of moral life, of a fully-lived life, is freedom from material necessity, which, moreover, the Greeks associated with the private realm, with the household, the realm which is subject to biological and material constraints. It's only when you get beyond that, that you can really, in any sense, talk about a sense of self, a personal identity or civic life. A moral life is a life that's lived in public.

Ignatieff: So you don't have life lived in a public domain. You have a life stripped down to bare essentials, to survival. Now Cornelius, you're a practising analyst. Does this portrait of the modern self ring a bell as a man who meets the modern self on the couch Monday through Friday?

Castoriadis: I think what is implied in all this is various things. 'One day at a time,' if I take this very nice expression, is what I call the lack of project. And this is for the individual and for society itself. Because 30 years ago, 60 years ago, irrespectively people on the Left would talk to you about the glorious night of the revolution, and people on the Right would talk to you about indefinite progress and so on and so forth. And now nobody dares express a grandiose or even moderately reasonable project which goes beyond the budget or the next elections. So there is a time horizon.

Now, in this respect you may say that survival is an expression you may criticise, because of course everybody thinks about his retirement pension and thinks also about his children's education and that the children could get a university degree or a technical degree and all this. But this time horizon is private. Nobody participates in a public time horizon, in the same way as nobody participates, again with the new qualifications, in a public space. I mean, we always participate in public space, but take the Place de la Concorde or Piccadilly Circus, or in New York I don't know, at the time of a jam, there you have one million people who are drowned in an ocean of social things, who are social beings, this is a social resort, and they are absolutely isolated, they hate each other and if they could open their way by neutronising the cars in front of them they would. I mean, today public space is what? It is within every home with TV precisely. But what is this public space?

Ignatieff: It's empty.

Castoriadis: It's empty or worse in a certain sense. It's public space mostly for publicity, for pornography — and I don't mean only straightforward pornography, I mean there are philosophers who are in fact pornographers, you know. Philosophy and so on and so forth.

Ignatieff: Then the question arises which I think is interesting: is this a cause or a consequence of the breakdown of the public realm? What's the relationship here between the self and the public realm in its crisis? Christopher?

Lasch: It strikes me that we live, not in a solid world. It's often said that consumer society surrounds us with things and encourages us to pay too much attention to things, but in a way I think that's also misleading. We live in a world that seems to be extremely unstable, to consist of fleeting images, a world that increasingly, thanks in part, I think, to the technology of mass communications, to acquire a kind of hallucinatory character. A kind of fantastic world of images, as opposed to a world of solid objects that can be expected to outlast one's own lifetime. What has waned perhaps is the sense of living in a world that existed before oneself and will outlast oneself. That sense of historical continuity which is provided by, among other things, simply a solid sense of palpable material things, seems to be increasingly mediated by this onslaught of images, often ones that appeal by design to our fantasies. Even science, I think, which was assumed in an earlier period to be one of the principal means of promoting a more rational and common-sensical view of the world, appears to us in daily life as a succession of technological miracles that makes everything possible. In a world where everything is possible, in a sense nothing is possible. And furthermore the boundaries between the self and the surrounding world tend to become increasingly indistinct.

Ignatieff: What I hear you saying there is almost a definition of the public realm. I mean, one of the things that you're saying is the public realm is the domain of historical continuity. In fact, in our culture it's very much the domain now of the media. The media gives us the public domain, a world of hallucinating images whose time frames are very short. They come and go. Their correspondence to reality is very problematic and public life looks like a kind of fantasy, a kind of dream world. But that doesn't get to the question I asked, which has to do with this business of causes and consequences. I'm wondering whether, Cornelius, you could pick that one up? What's the relationship between the self we've described and the crisis of the public domain that we've been talking about?

Castoriadis: I think it is not proper to search for a cause and a consequence. I think that the two things go together. I mean, development or changes in society are ipso facto changes in the structure of individuals, the way they act, the way they behave. After all, everything is social. But society as such has no address. I mean, you can't meet it. It's in you, in me, in the language, in the books, in the contraptions and so on and so forth. But I would say first, that there is one thing which one ought to stress in this respect, which is the disappearance of real social and political conflict and struggle.

Ignatieff: Why disappearance? That would strike me as odd.

Castoriadis: I don't see any. I don't see any. I see what happened in the States, where, take the classical example, the young blacks in the sixties would enter the centre of the cities and burn the stores and so on and so forth. And then you have the end of the seventies, the beginning of the Reagan era, you have ten per cent general unemployment, which means 20 per cent for the blacks and 48 per cent for young blacks, and these young blacks stay quiet. Now, I don't say that they ought to go and to burn, but they stay quiet! You have the situation in France now where people are thrown out of their job, they stay quiet. In Britain you have this tragedy of the miners, which I don't want to discuss, but anyhow, it was a sort of last flame of something which obviously is dying. And the thing is not difficult to understand, I think, because people feel, and rightly so, that political ideas which are in the political market as it exists now are not worth fighting for. And they also think that trade unions are more or less self-serving bureaucracies or lobby organisations.

Now, I think that this social and political conflict was extremely important. I mean, contrary to the Marxist commonplace, the history of society is not the history of class struggle. Usually the slaves and oppressed and the poor peasants and so on and so forth have stayed there and have accepted exploitation and oppression, and have benedicted the czars, you know. The problem of our world, of the Western world, the European world, was precisely this internal dynamic, this conflict, this putting into question of society. And this has brought about what I would call the dual character of Western societies. Marxists called them strictly capitalist societies, this is one aspect. The other aspect is that they are also societies where from the 12th century on the struggles for emancipation, for democracy, for limitation of the powers of the state and so on and so forth, have sedimented in institutions, you know, anthropological types, which are not the subject of the Czar or of the Emperor of China or of the Aztec emperor. There were these two elements.

And this second element, the element of struggle, during the whole period in 19th century, and up to 1914 or to 1930, took mostly the form of the working class movement, and also of the first and more genuine wave of the feminist movement. Because the true feminist movement is not Betty Friedan, it is the first girl who dared to go to a university and study medicine and see male corpses nude, despite what the family would say, and the first woman who entered a trade union and this is 1880. Now, this woman — let me finish — this woman somehow or other failed through Bolshevik totalitarianism on the one hand, through Social Democratic adaptation to capitalism on the other. And everything happens as if people were drawing the conclusion of all this that nothing is to be done, therefore we retrench ourselves. And this corresponds to the intrinsic movement of capitalism, expanding markets, built-in obsolescence and so on and so forth, and more generally expansion of mastery over people, not only as producers, but also as consumers.

Ignatieff: But I'd be one of those people who'd say you're prejudging the outcome of the struggle. What do you think?

Lasch: I was just going to add that under these conditions, politics becomes increasingly a question of interest groups, each presenting its rival claims to a share in the welfare state, defining its interests in the narrowest possible terms and deliberately eschewing any larger claims, or the attempt to state the claims of a group in universal terms.

One of the examples that you mentioned earlier, Cornelius, the black struggle in the United States, offers a good example of this, and also an example of the way in which often seemingly radical, militant revolutionary ideologies in our recent times have actually contributed to this process. The civil rights movement of the late fifties and sixties was in many ways a throwback, I think, to an earlier conception of democracy. It articulated the goals of blacks in a way that appealed to everybody. It attacked racism. Not just white racism, but racism. The black power movement, starting in the mid-sixties, which seemed to be much more militant and attacked Martin Luther King and other leaders of the early stage of this movement as bourgeois reactionaries, actually redefined the goals of the black movement, black power, an attack on white racism, as if racism was only a white phenomenon, in ways that made it much easier in the long run to redefine blacks in America as essentially another interest group claiming its share in the pie and not making any larger claims at all. I think that's one reason for the decline of militancy among American blacks.

Ignatieff: And I think, just to extend that analogy into the British case, one of the arguments about the miners' strike, which you brought up, was that it failed precisely because it was unable to present itself as anything other than a sectional claim. And that, had it been able to develop a language which said 'the miners' struggle is everyone's struggle,' then we might have had a different outcome than we actually had. Which is not to say they didn't try to do that, but that for very complicated reasons that public claim failed to convince other constituencies.

We can't take the miners' strike further here but I think we can use it as an example of something very important and interesting, which is the difficulty that groups in society have in presenting and speaking for and on behalf of the public interest. There's a sense which Christopher was expressing earlier that politics has fractured into interest groups, and if we're talking about a crisis of the public realm, that's what we mean. We mean that people only speak on behalf of themselves, they don't speak on behalf of the collectivity.

I mean, why is this going on? Why is this happening? That's what we need to understand. Do you have any thoughts Christopher?

Lasch: Well, it has something to do with the waning of any kind of public language, in order to make demands, to present demands as anything other than specific interests advanced by very specific groups of claimants, or victims too . . part of this, I think, has to do with the kind of moral elevation of the victim and the increasing tendency to appeal to victimisation as the only recognisable standard of justice. If you can prove that you've been victimised, discriminated against, the longer the better, that becomes the basis of claims, again that are made by very specific groups which assume that their own history is highly specific, has little reference to that of other groups or to the society as a whole, which doesn't figure in its language at all, and which furthermore, cannot even be understood by other groups. Again the illustration of the black movement is instructive, because, not to date this too precisely, beginning in the mid-sixties blacks and their spokesmen in America began to insist as a kind of article of faith that nobody else could even understand their history.

Castoriadis: Or the feminists. You can't understand women unless —

Lasch: Exactly, unless you're a woman — well, unless you're a woman first of all.

Lasch: Yeah, that's a fairly exact parallel, it seems to me. And when this happens, the possibility of a language that is understood by everybody and constitutes the basis of public life and political conversation is almost by definition ruled out.

Castoriadis: If you allow me, earlier you mentioned, between the lines, without naming him, Aristotle. Aristotle in his *Politics* mentions a wonderful Athenian law, which was that whenever the discussion in the assembly was about questions which could entail war with a neighbouring city the inhabitants of the respective frontier zone were excluded from the vote. Now, this is the Greek conception of politics, and this I stand for, in principle.

Lasch: And it's the very opposite of the modern —

Castoriadis: It's the very opposite. Imagine a disposition in the American constitution saying whenever problems concerning predominantly cotton-producing states come in discussion in the Senate the respective senators are excluded from the vote. But this is how it ought to be. And the whole political liberal conception — this has deep roots in 17th century political philosophers, you know, if you leave Rousseau aside — is the conception (a) that politics is to defend yourself against the state. It's not that we oppose ourselves as a political community, no, there is the Leviathan there, the monarch and then the state and so on, and we try to extract some freedom, some liberty, some rights. And (b), in as far as you succeed in that, we have all this bargaining between each other, the interest groups, and that's the representation and so on and so forth, and this ends up with the political society being fragmented just in the interests which the representatives are supposed to represent.

Ignatieff: This is a critique of liberal interest-based democracy. Is that one you share?

Lasch: One way of answering this might be to say that in the 18th century, 19th century, there were still at least remnants of earlier traditions opposed to liberalism in many important ways, though often assimilated to liberalism too in a confusing way. For example, the tradition of civic republican thought, which goes all the way again back to Aristotle and was revived in the 16th century in Florence.

Castoriadis: Also among new founding fathers. Jefferson was certainly not thinking of the polity as a combination of opposing interests.

Ignatieff: So what do you say, let me ask the sceptical question again, what do you say to people who would argue that those kinds of conceptions of the public good and the public interest that you find in civic republicanism, that you find in a very different form, as you say, in the early working class movement, those visions of the public good just don't appeal, don't speak, don't face up to the reality of the kind of society we live in now? That is, we live in a society simply too divided, too conflictual, too large, we're too far away from the Athenian city state, or even from the New England town meeting, these are traditions which are noble ones but they're lost. They're gone, they're vanished.

Lasch: I think it's significant, just to refer to this example one more time, that the civil rights movement in America drew so heavily, and I think fruitfully, on the biblical tradition in particular. Its ideas and language were saturated with that particular tradition and one can't imagine the movement without it. That suggests that in some parts of our societies perhaps these traditions are not altogether dead. There's very little in contemporary culture that encourages them, or is likely to elicit that kind of language or that conception of politics, but it still may be not as attenuated as we tend to assume.

Castoriadis: There has been a historical shift. I mean there have been two times in history — one in ancient Greece, in a limited way, another, in modern Europe, also in a limited way, which went on expanding up to a point, say up to 1914 or up to 1930 — where a huge change suddenly happened, both in the institutions of society and in the psychic set-up of individuals. And this change was, briefly speaking, that though in the previous situation you had what I call a heteronomous society, that is, nobody could even think that he could question the law, or the tribal representation of the world, suddenly people — suddenly within quotation marks, but it is suddenly — in the 7th or 6th centuries start asking is the law just?

And they built on this democracy. And they start asking do these gods exist? And they start building philosophy. Then the thing gets covered up and then starts again at the end of the Middle Ages, one must say with the proto-bourgeoisie which again reconstitutes political communities, polities, but by claiming some rights from the monarch, the church or the feudal lord. And that we still have, in a certain sense. And then of course it gathers momentum and goes much beyond what the Greeks would have dreamt of.

Now, where does this desire come from? I think it's a possibility of the human being, I don't think it's fatality. A much more fruitful question would be — and a question impossible to answer at the same time — where do we stand now? How many of the 55 million Englishmen, 55 million Frenchmen, 230 million Americans and so on and so forth, are really willing to act responsibly in order to take on their own fate? That's the problem. Do they have this desire or do they prefer to go on opening their fridge and looking at their TV?

Lasch: Let me suggest another possible line of reasoning that won't be so easily misread as an appeal to a kind of historical catastrophism. It's also possible that the private satisfaction that it has been the ultimate claim of the liberal state in the West to satisfy, with some reason, will increasingly be perceived as so empty and trivial that the appeal, the sort of historic appeal of such regimes will weaken on that side as well. Here we seem to have not so much a breakdown of public order — and I think there's plenty of evidence to suggest that the private satisfactions on which everything rides, in a sense, in a liberal regime, are beginning to wear pretty thin in themselves. Personal relationships, for example, are becoming increasingly thin and precarious. Family life suffers. There's a great deal of talk about returning to family values and so on, and while that seems to me to be misguided in many ways, it does I think evince a growing dissatisfaction right in the middle of the most affluent societies, and ones that have come closest to satisfying private needs and desires on a wide scale are no longer seen as doing this very effectively. And this is a criticism, not so much of the state, but of the quality of private life in modern society.

Castoriadis: On this I think you are perfectly right. I mean, I would say there are three levels to this. In a somehow arrogant way, I would say, first there is the reality, or the truth of the matter. The truth of the matter is that this increasing consumption and increasing satisfaction with private life is an increasing nothing, is something which is increasingly flat and increasingly empty. And on this you have said some very good things, I think, in your last book, about the quality of things. Nobody talks about the quality of things. People get things, but what is the quality of these things? And not just the quality from the user's point of view. I mean, a German philosopher would say 'these things have no thingness'. These plastic objects are not real objects. And that is true. I compare the toys I have to buy for my little daughter and the toys I had when I was a child, they are worlds apart. And also for relationships. There perhaps you could revert to what you asked me before, in my capacity as psychoanalyst, about the quality of relationships. I mean, all this going and doing and sleeping and having affairs and so on and so forth, how little has to do with true sexual satisfaction and/or with true love. Now, this is the reality. Again, from the point of view of an arrogant observer who says 'I know what's the reality.'

Now, there's a second point: how people perceive it. That's difficult. Do they perceive it like that? Are they satisfied? We live in societies where we still have the after-effects of upward mobility, therefore people can't compare with their childhoods which were much more miserable, or the lives of their parents and so on and so forth. And third, again, I insist, dissatisfaction can lead anywhere. Is not a part of the law and order movement in the States coming from the fact that people are fed up with what's going on? Even if they are themselves hypocritical?

Ignatieff: There seems to be another issue as well that's closely connected to that, which gets back to some of your earlier formulations, Christopher, which is that the theory that consumption satisfies, that the refrigerators and the cars and the TV sets give people happiness, presupposes a certain kind of self, a self that chooses, that rejects certain goods and takes other goods. The sovereign consumer. I mean, it seems to me what's underlying your view of it is simply that these goods are coming into a kind of empty centre. You know, there's no one on the bridge. There's no one on the deck of these little ships. And that's the thing that strikes you, I think.

Lasch: Yes, the notion of the sovereign consumer is a good way, I think, of getting at some of this. It presupposes an individual who's in a position to make discriminating use of increasing technological possibilities and so forth instead of being driven by them. And the sad thing is that consumerism, considered as a culture, not just as an abundance of commodities, seems to result in a situation where people are absolutely driven by their fantasies.

Castoriadis: Or by very passing external stimuluses, like a publicity ad or something like that. The fad of the moment.

Ignatieff: And all of this mocks the idea of the sovereign individual which is the basis, very much, of political liberalism itself as well? But that takes us, I think, back to this minimal self, and I think this is the moment to look much more closely at it. The word narcissism, for example, the narcissist self, has been thrown around here and I'm just wondering, as an analyst, what you'd say to this concept. Can we get closer to why it is that this self is empty? Why it is that this self is unable to choose? Why it is that this self seems void of purpose?

Castoriadis: The self-image. Who am I? A question without end. But there can be no society which does not give an answer to this question of the singular person: who am I? And it's not enough to say 'you are Cornelius Castoriadis, aged so and so, place of birth,' I mean it's not that. You have to be something substantive. And this is essentially connected with the other thing which the institution of society must provide individuals: a meaning, or a framework of meaning for their life. And this is in very deep crisis again today. Because the 'who am I?', the man or the woman — the woman certainly will not reply 'I'm an honest housewife who prepares nice food for her husband and brings up her children in the proper way and teaches them to read the gospel.' She will not reply that. And she doesn't know what she is. And if the woman doesn't know who she is, then of course the man doesn't know who he is. But also the man doesn't know who he is because he will not say with pride 'I am, at General Motors, and I earn so much.' Who can say that? Very few people. So, there is this crisis of identity in this sense of a correspondence of a social predelineated role or possibilities of role, which the subject can invest or cathect, can positively value and address itself, which is one of the components of the crisis we are talking about today.

Ignatieff: I feel we ought to try and tighten up some of these things in a sense. I think the thing that's been said very clearly is something interesting, which is that the self, the constitution of the identity of each individual person, is a political issue. Societies which fail to give people a vernacular of roles, a set of identities that are stable, that are firm, that allow them to sustain hard times, is a society that's failing its individuals. That seems to me the core of what we're saying.

What kind of selves can we invent? I mean, what kind of political theory of the self can we start constructing? Because it seems to me, if you take the example of the woman, the housewife who has gone through 15 years of feminism and thinks 'by god, that's not a role I want,' or a husband tied into a job which doesn't allow him any time with his kids and thinks 'by god, that's not a role I want. I want to be a father, I don't want to be just a producer of money,' you see all across society people struggling with roles that society has ascribed them. So how do you reconcile that freedom to struggle for a self, to struggle free of old selves, how do you reconcile that with the thing we all feel is missing, which is a common language of what the self ought to be? That is, how do you reconcile the freedom of an individual to choose his self in some way, to make himself, with a society which has a common language of selfhood?

Lasch: I think it's a little misleading to talk of individuals who are free to choose an identity or to make a self. I think it's very important to insist on the degree to which people are never free in this respect. The degree to which people are, often in ways they're not even aware of, captives of many things. Of a past. Nobody is without a past, even though our society encourages us to deny that. And nobody has carte blanche to make an identity. That's one of the illusions, I think, that our current ideologies tend to foster. So that there needs to be also an acknowledgement of limits of the degree to which people are not free, in this sense, to sort of choose interchangeable identities. And furthermore, to change these identities on a sort of weekly basis. I don't know what the answer to your question is, but it does seem to me that it has something to do with holding that in mind as well as the freedom to choose. The freedom not to be restricted by imposed social roles.

Ignatieff: But couldn't you then put the question another way and say, 'okay, you must be right that we can't have a kind of promiscuous discarding, shuffling off of identities because human beings aren't snakes, they're people with pasts and histories and they don't shuffle off their identities like skin? Okay, but can't you speak of character then?' What I pick up in a lot of your thinking is a sense, a very old traditional sense, of character. That is, that we can't prescribe identities. It'd be foolish to. It'd be impossible in this kind of society. But a society can say what kind of character it respects and admires. It can say, 'this is the kind of person we honour, we respect.' And maybe that's where public language has to go.

Castoriadis: But, Michael, it must strike you that the words you just pronounced would be ridiculous perhaps for seven-tenths of the audience.

Ignatieff: Possibly. We'll have to see.

Castoriadis: Honour and respect? I mean, this is one of the problems, the image of the self holds because others recognise it and in a certain sense approve it. And this is a necessary, you know, pinning of this image. Now, this precisely, with the crumbling of the public world, means also that what Hegel was calling 'recognition' or what you would call respect has no meaning whatever. I mean, it's just the vedettes, the stars, which are there for a season and then they are lost.

Ignatieff: But how far are we going to push that kind of moral pessimism? I mean, are both of you saying there's simply no place for moral leadership in a society like ours? All we've got is Andy Warhol's, 'you'll be a star for 15 minutes.' We no longer have a society where somebody can get up and say 'look, I just think there's certain kinds of character that are worthy of esteem and certain kinds of character that are not.' And I would challenge the contention that seven-tenths of this audience — who knows what they think? But let me make the assumption that a society can't function without a certain ground level sense of human character — that you don't lie, that you don't cheat, that you don't steal. You try and be a good father, a good mother.

Castoriadis: I would be very happy if I were wrong. And if the audience were totally in agreement with you. But I would also hope that they would raise some problems. And that's precisely the rub. You said one has to be a good father and good mother. But what is it today to be a good father or a good mother? I mean, when I was a child a good father was a father who would forbid his daughter, for instance, to go out after 8 o'clock in the evening till she was 20 or 22 at least, or even later, without a chaperone. All right, is this today a good father? I mean, the problem goes deeper. Even if people agree that standards of decency, of honesty, of morality, as I hope they do agree, are absolutely indispensable for a society to live, there is a tremendous problem. And this is why I say that the whole business is ambiguous — this is also positive — there is a question mark about what it is. I mean, we do not accept a patriarchal father. We do not accept a patriarchal husband. And I think we are right. But in these new conditions what does it mean to be a married man and what does it mean for the woman? Has the woman to work at the same time? And then who is doing the washing and do you share, and is this a solution?

Ignatieff: I'm not appealing to some generalised moral intuition that we're all supposed to share, but I do think that one of the consequences of the kind of debates that we're having tonight, that have been going on at least since the early sixties, is a very intense discussion about how far freedom to choose yourself, to make yourself, to choose your own values, at what point that has to give way to a sense of collective social obligations, to a sense of what it is that human beings ought to have.

Castoriadis: But, Michael, you see, you spoke about freedom, and this is a very important point. Why freedom is not an easy thing and an easy concept. In a certain sense, if you speak about true freedom, it's, I would say, a tragic concept. Like democracy's a tragic regime. Because there are no external limits and there are no mathematical theorems which tell you when you stop. And a democracy is also the same thing. Democracy is a regime where we say 'we make our own laws on the base of our own mind.' Or our common morality. But this morality, even if it were to coincide, I say this to my crypto-christian friend Christopher Lasch, even if it was to coincide with the laws of Moses, or with the gospel, it is not because it is in the laws of the gospel, it is because we, as a polity, accept it, endorse it and say thou shalt not kill. Right? The authority does not come from god, even if 90 per cent of the society are believers and believe that the authority of the commandment comes from god, for the political society the authority does not come from god. It comes from the decision of the citizens.

Now, the citizens are sovereign. Where is this sovereignty limited? You have a saying in English public law that Parliament, that supposedly the people, can do anything except transform a man into a woman, I think. That is, the biological is the limit. Now we know that the biological starts becoming plastic. But that means that the British Parliament could tomorrow decide that blonde people have no right to vote. Nothing objects to that. It doesn't. I mean, the British have a democratic tradition. There are no external limits, and that's why democracy can perish and has perished at times in history, like a tragic hero. A tragic hero in Greek tragedy does not perish because there was a limit and he transgressed it. The tragic hero perishes out of hubris. That is, because he transgresses in a field where there are no foreknown limits. And that's our plight. I mean, if we are free we decide individually and collectively about our laws and nobody can tell us. We decide what is right and wrong.

Ignatieff: I think the mention of the word tragedy provides us with a moment to end. The sense that human morality is human choice, collective choice, that human life is a question of choosing and making tragic choices between values with no one to define the limits beforehand, is I think a good place to stop. I think this whole discussion has been dominated by two figures really: by the figure of Aristotle in a way, and also by the figure of Freud. It's dominated by the figure of Aristotle in the sense that we began with an idea of the public realm which we've inherited from our oldest traditions, a sense that a human being cannot become a human being in full until he or she becomes a citizen, shares in a collective life with the public realm. And that's the tradition we start from. It's the tradition that haunts us. The second figure that's been throughout this discussion has been Freud, with a sense of the self, the modern self, which poses very, very acute questions to that classical political tradition. Through Freudian theory, through psychoanalytic theory, as Christopher Lasch and Cornelius Castoriadis have adapted it, one

gets a very thought-provoking hypothesis to the effect that we are
no longer producing selves in this kind of society capable of realising
the Aristotelian vision. And that's one of the messages tonight. It's
a difficult question. Have we become different kinds of people?
Have we lost that ideal? And that's where I think we'll leave it.

CHAPTER 4

The Post-Industrial Society

Michael Ignatieff
with Daniel Bell, Emma Rothschild and Ulrich Briefs

Ignatieff: 25 years ago the post-industrial society was just the image of a distant future. Now that future is already here. The personal computer, microchip technology, fibre optics, lasers, software, hardware, bits and bytes. 25 years ago the locomotives of our economy were steel, automobiles and petrochemicals. Now the driving force is computer and information technology. Tonight we examine where this new future is leading us. The choices for our children seem stark: assembling microcircuits for some Japanese multinational or serving hamburgers for some American multinational. It looks like there will be a high-tech, high wage future for the few, a no-tech, low wage future for some, and unemployment for many. The industrial revolution replaced the jobs it destroyed, but the post-industrial revolution seems to be destroying the jobs it replaces. The political dilemma is cruel. If we modernise, we lose jobs. If we fail to modernise, we lose jobs too. At stake is not just jobs, but our politics, our culture and our values. Are we going to be the masters of our future, or merely its victims? Are we going to ride the tiger of change or end up inside it? 25 years ago Daniel Bell of Harvard University coined the term 'post-industrial society' and set the terms for the debate we've been having ever since. He's with us tonight. To debate his thesis we have Emma Rothschild, an economist at MIT and Ulrich Briefs, senior researcher for the German trade union movement. Daniel Bell, I thought I'd start with you, tell me what you mean by post-industrial society.

Bell: First, I would not say I was predicting the future or projecting the future. I don't think anyone can do that. I was trying essentially to sketch the logical construct of new principles of organisation and new ways of life which might be possible if some of these things came into being. We know, for example, we had an agrarian way of life and for most of Western society that's vanished although the products are here. We all need food, but there's no agrarian way of life and fewer and fewer people, three per cent or less in the United Kingdom, three per cent or less in the United States, produce that food. In the same way, the manufacturing sectors, as you've indicated, have begun to shrink. To some extent they're moving out of the Western world, so as a whole they're not completely shrinking, but in the Western world they are shrinking as sectors of employment and as sectors of importance. Therefore, my problem was, as I first thought about it, what new elements might be coming into being and what are the sources of it? I therefore tried to establish it as a logical construct. Fundamentally, I would say it is this: there is a new principle which underlies the new technology. It's not simply the extension of the old.

And that I think is the radical difference which is still not well understood, namely that the new technology derives from the codification of theoretical knowledge. Now, all human societies have always existed on the basis of knowledge, but most of the inventions we've had and most of the industries we've had: steel, automobiles, electricity, came in the 19th century — although steel begins perhaps earlier in the coking process of Abraham Derby — but basically these were done by talented tinkerers, whereas if one looks today at the new technology they derive from work in theoretical physics. A paper by Einstein in 1904 on the photoelectric effect is the basic progenitor of work which led to the laser, which simply is the light amplification stimulated by the emission of radiation. A theoretical model by Felix Bloch of the lattice structure of matter created the basis of the transistor. So that inevitably there's a very radical new joining of science and technology and that becomes an important principle. When you come to the more manifest and overt aspects, it seems to me essentially that you have a new intellectual technology replacing machine technology, but equally you have a shift to services.

I would disagree somewhat, and I suspect we'll have to come back to that more and more, with the rather rapid bifurcation you made regarding the amount of jobs and the way it happens. Increasingly, in every modern society, you have multiplication of a variety of jobs. The dictionary of occupational titles in the United States lists 22,000 titles. Services is not just fast food franchises or microchips. Services are often human services. In fact, the largest expansion of jobs is in human services, health and education. The real question is can we have the productivity and generate the productivity to pay for those? Because they become increasingly necessary in a modern society. There are a large number of jobs possible, there are huge potentials. The question is where do you get the productivity to pay for them? That, it seems to me, becomes the direct economic question. Then I go back to my scheme of a post-industrial society, I would say it's essentially an attempt to identify these principles which involve theoretical knowledge as a fundamental element, a shift to different kinds of services as a framework for jobs in society.

Ignatieff: Let me ask you just before I go to Ulrich Briefs for comment, if you look at this post-industrial future, what's the issue there that worries you most? Where's the neuralgic point, the thing we've got to worry about?

Bell: I think the issue is one of those you put forward, but I would not be as pessimistic about the potential. The issue of inclusion and exclusion. That is, society may exclude certain kinds of people who are unable to have the necessary skills to function in that kind of society. I think that's a very real problem. It also of course widens the advanced industrial societies as against other societies which may not be able, for a whole variety of political reasons — political stability, cultural reasons — to come into these phases, or may not be able to take up the slack of industrial work which many of these countries have tried to do. So that the increasing divisions between advanced industrial societies and what's called the Third World — which is not a useful term any more because Asia is to a large extent part of an advanced industrial scheme — but that kind of division, and internally the divisions between those who are capable of functioning in areas of the new society and those who are not, seems to me become the areas of friction.

Ignatieff: Ulrich Briefs, that's the thesis, what do you make of it?

Briefs: Well, first I agree with the fact that there is something changing in a very profound way in our society. There's no doubt about this. And it has of course something to do with the broad range of new technologies which you quoted in the beginning. But I'm entirely different in opinion with regard to the possible or probable outcomes of this development. I think that we are still in the very old-fashioned and still powerfully existing capitalist society. I think that the economic contradictions which are already existing in our societies, in the highly developed societies of the West, will not be solved by this development but will be aggravated. Look at what has been going on in the last ten or fifteen years throughout the Western world. Let me quote only a few figures from Western Europe. We had, at the beginning of the seventies, throughout the countries of Western Europe, at that time already one of the highly developed parts of the world, about 2.5 million people unemployed. We now have more than 15 million, if we only take account of part of the hidden reserve army, industrial reserve army, so to speak, the army of the unemployed. Look at the giant excess capacities which we have nowadays, in steel, in automobile manufacturing, in other sectors.

Ignatieff: Ulrich, what do you mean by excess capacity?

Briefs: Excess capacities means that we have been, throughout the last ten, fifteen years especially, but this has also been a development from the period before, establishing a giant productive apparatus which to an increasing degree apparently can no longer be fully used. That's a fact, and it's one of the striking facts in this context. And I think that gives also a few gloomy hints with regard to the future development. The fact that, for instance, in West Germany, and I think it's a similar situation in Great Britain or in France or even in the US or even in Japan, that even some of the most modern parts of this productive apparatus can no longer be used. That's one of the striking features. This indicates, for instance, that all these modernisation projects apparently do not lead towards a solution of our economic problems. On the third side we have to sort of look at least to the fact that in a giant amount we have idle capital floating around through the world. In the beginning of the seventies, the amount of idle capital floating around was estimated to be about 350 billion US dollars. It is now estimated at beyond 2,000 billion US dollars. And I think this, especially also in view of certain parallels to the twenties and thirties, must give us some alarming signs. I mean, the contradictions. People fully capable to produce, the reserve army of the unemployed, in Western Germany more than one million people, qualified, skilled workers, even engineers, even medical doctors are now unemployed. On the other hand, machinery, fully usable capacities, facilities, which can no longer be used. And the third point, money, idle capital floating around in giant sums. And what we see is that apparently the combinatorial power of our economic system is not sufficient, is not capable of bringing these so-called factors of production together.

Ignatieff: We've got already two differently inflected scenarios, two differently inflected versions of what's happening here. I'm just wondering if whether we could bring in Emma Rothschild at this point, not to arbitrate, but to add a comment of her own.

Rothschild: Well, I think to some extent the divergence corresponds to a divergence between what's been happening in Western Europe and what's been happening in the United States. I think the experience of the US since 1973, the miracle of US job creation in the private sector, has a really fascinating relationship to the development of the post-industrial society and to the projections which have proved impressively accurate that were put forward in Professor Bell's book and in many studies of the US Department of Labour at that time and subsequently. There has been massive job creation in private services in the US. Much of it has been in those services which are based on intellectual technology and on what some economists call human capital, but there has at the same time been an absolute explosion of employment in services which demand really very few skills, which perhaps demand human contacts but not any sort of access to the advanced technologies that you mentioned at the beginning.

Ignatieff: Could you give an example here?

Rothschild: Well, I'm thinking that there are really three industries which have been responsible for the bulk of the job creation boom in the States. They are private health services, which now employ about six million people, business services which employ about four million people, and they're not all things like data processing, a lot are, for example, what's called 'services to buildings', which is quite often janitors. A lot of it is temporary help services. And the third, and in many ways the particularly interesting one, is what's called 'eating and drinking places', bars, restaurants, some of them Macdonalds, but not only franchises, and that employs over five million people now. And it really does provide jobs which are more remote from the new technologies you've been talking about than almost any other sector of the economy.

Bell: But they're interrelated in this respect, I mean, no one would ever dream of saying there's a single cause which is creating this whole round wave of things. There are large social and structural changes in the American society, the most important one, of course, being the change in the role of women in the labour force. In 1950 you found that 70 per cent of the persons in the labour force were men whose wives were at home with two children. Today that's down to 15 per cent. Now, once you have large numbers of women working in the labour force you're going to have a demand for services such as fast foods or dry cleaning services or laundry services etc. So the question that comes in is, are these jobs satisfactory? Most of them are not. What kind of problems are created by them? And I think the point that Miss Rothschild is making is a crucial one. You have had a multiplication of new jobs, and I think most strikingly they come in small enterprises and small businesses. In almost every area where these areas expand, the unit size of enterprise goes down. Which means that people increasingly work in unit sizes of under 500 persons. The idea of the large plants of Ford, the big plants of Boeing, are essentially archaic. Even in the manufacturing plants, General Motors and General Electric now find it's more effective to start smaller plants. More than that, more importantly than that, the work of some colleagues of Emma Rothschild, Charles Sable and Michael Piori, shows that increasingly the new kinds of production if it's going to survive is going to be specialised, flexible, small batch, mini mills in steel, customised production. The old era, if we're talking again in a larger framework, the old era of mass-production, mass-consumption societies, will pass, not overnight — some of it may go to the Orient — but increasingly in the advanced technological sectors what you're going to have are smaller unit enterprises and therefore new kinds of work. Take, for example, the whole expansion of software. You have the whole growth of microcomputers, which nobody ever imagined five years ago would spread as rapidly as it did. Microcomputers give a certain degree of access through mini and mainframe to databases, to information and such. It also means people have to have programmes that they can work with. But to write a programme is a very laborious thing. It takes something like 2,000 hours of work to write a software programme and a switching code, let's say, in a telecommunications system code, a million lines of code. The whole expansion of the software programming industry, much of it done on a kind of cottage industry type of work, has been a fascinating phenomenon. True, as a magnitude you say how much is it? Well, it's a few hundred thousand people, but, as you know, a few hundred thousand people here —

Ignatieff: But for you that's the growth point of the new economy?

Bell: It's a possible growth point. For me this kind of technology as with most technology can be used to centralise or decentralise, can be used to expand control or contract control. There's nothing indigenously which says it has to be one way, that's the crucial point.

Briefs: I'm sorry, really sorry about this because software development, well we all have had our hopes that this might give us a great relief with regard to the labour market. But in the Federal Republic, which is not the most unmodern country in this line in West Europe, there are exactly 6,000 jobs per year coming —

Bell: You don't have a computer industry.

Briefs: — in a very defined sense of software specialists.

Bell: You don't have a computer industry really. It's a small computer industry.

Briefs: No, that's not right. It's relatively small compared to the US industry. But, for instance, IBM West Germany is the largest international subsidiary of IBM. But just blunt figures, Daniel Bell, I think we simply have to see things as they are. We have had a growth of 300 per cent in value terms throughout the last 12 years, with IBM Germany, with Nixdorf, with Siemens and so on, which are very competitive, especially Nixdorf.

Ignatieff: But they haven't produced the jobs?

Briefs: But they have added only 70 per cent of jobs. Now everyone says 70 per cent, that's a lot. But they have added below 30,000 jobs and we need two millions. And just in order to show how adventurous it is even to devise in that direction any solution, let me quote one other even more sobering example, the microelectronics industry, and we are, with regard to some specific realms of production, still leading in the world, even there, has from '75 to '80 in West Germany witnessed an increase in production value from 3.4 billion deutschemark in '75 to 4.4 billion deutschemark in 1980, and employment receded by more than 8 per cent. They lost jobs. They didn't add, they lost. I mean, the picture is very blunt.

Rothschild: It is important to be clear that there aren't only two models. I think if one takes the average for Western Europe, my bifurcation was correct, but there certainly are countries which have been much more successful on a non-US model.

Ignatieff: Which?

Rothschild: One example is Japan, but I think, for example, of Sweden, in Western Europe, which has had unemployment, official unemployment, between two and three per cent and not that great an increment in training and labour market schemes. It doesn't have much excess capacity at the moment. And it happens also to be one of the countries with an extremely high rate of female labour force participation, an extremely high rate of unionisation of the labour force, and a union movement which has been very very strongly committed over a period of 20 or 30 years to modernisation, to the introduction of new technologies. And I think that the point that Michael made at the very beginning, about if we modernise we lose jobs, to some extent is contradicted by the, in many ways, really very positive experience of the private sector in Sweden where modernisation has produced jobs which basically are better and basically have led to export potential.

Bell: I would also add, if I may, the colleague of Emma Rothschild, namely Charles Sable, pointing to work in Italy, where the growth of what has been really a black economy has been an extraordinarily flourishing economy of small enterprises, of a new extraordinary initiative and being very productive.

Ignatieff: The difference here is that these are black economy industries that use high tech often.

Bell: High tech is a bad word here. High tech seems as if there's a sector called high tech and there's low tech. Not at all. The crucial thing about the new technology is it pervades all dimensions of industry. The automobile of the next ten years is going to be a very different automobile because of the introduction of the new technological features. Not just robotics, but various kinds of control devices through microprocessors in the organisation of the automobile itself in the production process. Textiles is being reorganised this way. There's one firm — I was just in Italy — I learned of the firm called Bennetton, which had been a black firm, so to speak, within the underground economy, it now has 1200 franchises, outlets, which are held together by an information system. And they have a totally-developed market system of knowing what's going to move and what doesn't move. Total inventory control. If something isn't moving in a week they simply discard it by a quick sale. But it's held together, a franchise system of 1200 units organised by this Italian firm, now held together by a world-wide information system. Now that is high tech in a sense changing the character of an old industry.

Briefs: Let me add another textile story from West Germany. Some 15 years ago we had one of the largest industries in West Germany which was the textile and garments industry, having about 800,000 jobs. We now have a textile and garments industry with about 450,000 jobs, which economically is successful. It is, as far as I know, the second most successful, in terms of exportation and so on, after the Italians. But what does that teach? I think it has to teach us the story that apparently all these processes of reorganising an industry, in the sense in which Daniel Bell talked about it, this also incorporates some sort of high technology, but high technology corresponding to the long established history in the textile industry in West Germany, but we have half of the jobs. That's the point.

Ignatieff: You've lost half of the jobs.

Briefs: We have now half of the jobs. We have lost half of the jobs. By a thorough process of reorganisation, restructuring, and especially modernisation of our textile industry.

Bell: That may be a plus, that's not necessarily negative.

Briefs: We possibly have the most modern large-scale textile industry in Western Europe.

Bell: But that may be that you're very productive.

Briefs: And they are most of them — let me add one further word — they are mostly medium and small size firms, and and it did not prevent from cutting down by about half of the jobs.

Bell: But wouldn't the real social question be this: it's very good that you have it done by half the number of people because you're then getting more productivity. Where can you then use the people who've been displaced? Can you use them productively? Why keep them in this sense in an old industry if it's going to be a drag? I mean, that seems to be the crucial question. There's nothing wrong in losing jobs if you can, in this sense, use people elsewhere and use them productively. And can you therefore make a transition?

Briefs: I'm deeply sympathetic with the idea of creating new forms. I mean, I'm myself active within the Green movement in West Germany, so that indicates perhaps that we are driving forward, or trying, in a hard-core political way, to drive forward all sorts of different structures, creating all these small size workers-owned and alternative shops and so on. But it is not a solution to the giant economic problems and contradictions in which we are already and in which we will be in a much more aggravated form even in the future. That's the point.

Ignatieff: What we seem to be losing sight of slightly is the novelty of the times we're living through. These analogies backwards convey the impression that we're simply going through the existing difficulties of adjusting an industrial economy, when in a sense our starting point was very different. Our starting point was that something new is happening to this economy. There are structural changes in this economy which are wild cards in this game.

Bell: Can I give you what I think is the great novelty?

Ignatieff: What's the novelty?

Bell: And which I think — it's intangible, but it's the way I've thought about the nature of post-industrial life — namely, in a pre-industrial society life is a game against nature. It's basically extractive industries. People work on farms, on the soil, on the sea and mining. It's hazardous, subject to the vicissitudes of nature etc. And the character of work is shaped by this. So people are farmers or fishermen or timbermen or seamen. And that's been the character of work in most pre-industrial societies. So it's a game against nature. In an industrial society work has been, not for everybody but for basically a strong nucleus of people, what I'd call a game against fabricated nature. Namely, you're hitched to a machine and the pacing of work and the rhythms of work are dictated by the machine technology. And the image, of course, has been Charlie Chaplin with 'Modern Times'. But in that framework, it seems to me, in a post-industrial society work is a game between persons in which nature is excluded, things are excluded. And more and more, whether it be in large organisations, whether it be in the government bureaucracies or universities or research organisations or hospitals, work is a game between persons. And that is radically different in its psychology and its social psychology than other kinds of work. Now it's true that there have always been small numbers of persons, intellectuals and administrators who've lived this kind of work, but if you think of a society in which everybody is involved on this kind of basis then it seems to me radically different. Now, let me take two more seconds on this. I sometimes think of a man who gave me at least a clue to this, and that was Rousseau. In *Emile* he made a statement which is very fascinating because it goes against an aspect of the modern temper. Rousseau said in *Emile*, dependence upon things is freedom, dependence upon people is slavery. As you know, Rousseau always had this hyperbole to exaggerate these things. But what he meant essentially was obviously this: dependence upon things is freedom because you can walk away from things. Dependence upon people is slavery because you cannot walk away from people. Work of this sort therefore involves reciprocity. If work now involves more reciprocity it's no accident, so to speak, that you have things like encounter groups, sensitivity training, the emphasis on psychology today. Sometimes in an exaggerated way. But clearly, the sense of claiming rights, claiming equal rights, equal pay for equal work, the whole element of the women's movement is saying historically certain occupations have been kept in lower wages, why should a nurse be kept at a half the wage of a teamster, or a lorryman? These have been historical circumstances. But if we think of comparable worth, now it seems to me that the crucial aspect of a post-industrial society is people become much more aware of these elements. What do you get, what do I get? And it's no accident, it seems to me, that the crucial terms which are involved here is fairness and equity. And these are terms which increasingly become important in any sense of the character of work, because I do think, intangible as it is, there is this basic module of change between work as a game against nature, game against fabricated nature, and now as a game between persons. I realise this is a very large scheme, it's subject to all kinds of —

Rothschild: I'd like to try and make it —

Briefs: — It's now a game against men. Or a game against persons. Not among persons.

Ignatieff: Let Emma come in here.

Rothschild: I'd like to try and make it an even grander scheme. A game against nature, a game against fabricated nature, and now a game against inner nature. You started with the transition from agriculture to industry. And that was a tremendously important social convulsion which also had the advantage of giving what economists would call intra-sectoral positive effects to overall productivity growth. The fact that productivity was increasing in agriculture and people were going into industry helped. That was a big transition. And in a sense it came to an end in the US with what could be called perfect convergence, in that around 1980 the level of productivity in agriculture was exactly the same as the level of productivity in the rest of the economy. Maybe we're now seeing a new sort of divergence in which people leave the industrial economy for a low productivity service economy, low measured productivity, in which the intra-sectoral effects are negative. Namely, each person that leaves a job producing goods or producing something like electricity or producing communication services and goes to work in a fast food industry is contributing an adverse productivity effect, but also is going back in some ways to a more constrained way of life. One of the basic ideas of development economics is that the different sectors of an economy become more like each other over time. And this is Kuznets' view and it's to do with the perfection of markets and, going back to Adam Smith and to Marx, that you overthrow obstructions of custom and prejudice and people move freely from one sector to another. And the classic example of that is you go out of agriculture, which is constrained by relations to nature and history and geography and so on, into the industrial sector, which is relatively unconstrained. And you get this sectoral convergence in economic terms. Well, maybe we're now coming into a phase of divergence, in which people are moving again into a more constrained sort of activity. Only the constraints, partly they're old fashioned constraints, partly they're constraints to do with government regulations in favour of fairness, partly they're constraints of psychology, and that's why I say it's a game against inner nature. People simply don't want to eat, well like Aldous Huxley said 'panglandular biscuits' instead of cheeseburgers in a Macdonalds. They don't want to do what world fairs predicted. Namely, get dehydrated meals from a hole in the wall. They don't want, at least outside the US, they don't want some kind of privatisation and mechanisation of basic social services. So you're creating all sorts of new constraints and obstructions of over-development in a symmetrical way to the process of development out of agriculture.

Bell: May I respond? I think it's partly true, because these have become so much more diverse, but I think one can be mesmerised by the images of fast food and Macdonalds and not see more important developments. These are short run responses, and I think these industries themselves will change. But let me take one illustration of what I mean which, in economic terms, has been one of the most crucial problems. This is essentially the Western ageing population. In Germany you probably will have by the year 2000 almost no youth by then, almost everybody being an old person, but leave that aside as an economic problem.

Ignatieff: What a thought.

Bell: Well it's true, given their population trends.

Briefs: You're right.

Bell: Let alone what's happening now in North Africa and the rest of the world, where the youth population will be the big bulge. But if you have an ageing population, the kind of services that old people need are one-to-one services. The people who need caring, the whole notion of caring professions, as you have an ageing population, has been an enormous question for every society. And this is not mechanised, it's not fast food, it's a question of what do older people do when they need nursing home care, when they need post-operative care, when they need care which involves the kind of psychological stress and problems they have, particularly as you have the extension of life into the seventies and eighties of this sort?

And it seems to me this is a one-to-one kind of relationship increasingly, and therefore it's a very different tenor in the nature of work and the tenor of human relationships. So what I'm saying is that — I'm not trying to idealise any of these things, I'm trying to be, it seems to me, analytical about it — that fundamentally the relationships which increasingly will extend in Western societies will be ones which involve more and more personal ties of various kinds. And that, it seems to me, touches on the things you want to know, because, after all, Michael, you wrote a book called *The Needs of Strangers*. I think of it in a different sense. Max Weber, after all, who first thought about this, talked about a difference between *brothers* and *others*. He thought that capitalism is a world which went from tribal *brotherhood* to universal *otherhood* in this way. Well, in many ways we're now repersonalising the world. We're repersonalising it because in the nature of work we're becoming, I won't say brothers to one another, but essentially more and more tied to one another in ways in which we have to be aware of one another. Whether it be equity in pay, fairness in comparable worth, the psychological tensions of not aggravating a person by the way in which we treat the individual etc.

Ignatieff: I think, if I can just make a comment at this point, if you have a society that moves towards one-to-one relations in work — the example of care for the aged interests me a lot — where caring becomes one of the primary economic, social and personal relations with society, caring between strangers, that is between a person employed to take care of someone else's father or mother when they get old, I think one of the things that concerns me is how a society teaches caring as a moral disposition. Because it's one thing to teach a person to punch out metal on a die press, it's another to teach the dispositions of caring. I mean, it happens that we leave that to the family, in a sense, we leave it to a kind of sedimentary process of socialisation. But it does strike me more and more that if you move into a service-based society where caring and interpersonal relations are what matter, then a new social question comes onto the agenda, which is what the ancients would call the question of how we teach virtue.

Bell: Yes. Well, I think one answer, there's a very strong awareness of this, at least among some persons in the States, and it comes under a new phrase which is called 'the creation of mediating institutions.' We did have a movement from the family to social services, many of which became organised within state institutions, some of which was very good as social services, some of which became rather impersonal. In the United States, as we know, it became very drastically bad, because many of the social services became simply heavily bureaucratised and high cost and the delivery of services was very poor. The question is how do you come back to what may be called intermediate institutions? Community-based institutions? If it's no longer necessarily the family, it can be the church or can be more community-based institutions, voluntary associations etc, which have resources available to them. I think that's a double question. It's not only the question of what kinds of caring can people be taught, but can resources be made available to them? And how do you make those resources available to them? Instead of these being organised by state bureaucracies in terms of organised missions and programmes, how do you have neighbourhoods which have diverse needs, have resources made available to them? Because you have different neighbourhoods. Some neighbourhoods require more childcare, some require more old age care. The other question is what kind of basic restructuring of social units you have, with some control over resources to meet in a very direct way the kind of needs they have. Many years ago in a different respect, dealing with some economic problems, I made a statement I think a bit facile but I think essentially true, in which I said the nation states have become too small for the big problems of life and too big for the small problems of life. It's too small for the big problems of life because you don't have mechanisms of meeting the change in scale of international flows of economic organisation, economic flows of work, and too big for the small problems because it becomes unresponsive to the variety and diversity of local needs. And the real question is how does one restructure both levels of social organisation?

Briefs: I hate to do this, but our experience again has to be very sobering, because we have, for instance, been seeing that from the seventies onward the expansion of the public sectors which comprises also a considerable part of these caring activities, hospitals and teaching activities, the expansion has been stopped. So the idea to provide from this side the necessary relief for the shrinking of the industrial core sector, so to speak, did not materialise in reality.

Ignatieff: We've been talking about welfare and we've been talking about the expansion of the public sector and a marriage between the public and a private sector in the caring field, but haven't we missed out a huge area here, which takes us back to the problem that Ulrich Briefs doesn't want us to forget, which is we have 15 to 20 million people unemployed in the European economy at the moment? The pressure of that demand for unemployment insurance and social security is growing, it's a tremendous cost, it's estimated that the entire revenue from the North Sea oil bonanza in England is actually paid to keep the unemployed alive in this country. I mean, the costs of transition to a post-industrial society include tremendously high social costs of this kind. I mean, what do we need to do to change the welfare and social security systems to cope with an economy which may be running on persistently high levels of unemployment through the eighties and nineties?

Bell: I do think that there's a very real problem in the minds of many people, particularly middle class people, who feel that the costs of a welfare state have gone too high. Richard Rose of Strathclyde has asked 'can Britain go bankrupt?' Arthur Linbeck in Sweden, who'd been a social democrat or a socialist, now is coming out with a book saying the welfare state is simply too costly. You have the same arguments, Ulrich has pointed out, in Germany, which has restricted the growth of health expansion. And I think it probably is a very real question. But it's only a real question because it was put within the old frameworks. And it seems to me the real problem is essentially of two kinds. One, is there a possibility of matching the way in which the economies work? I think one of the problems comes from the fact, I mentioned it before in passing, that you have national political structures and more and more of an international economy. It becomes impossible for any single country increasingly to manage its own fate, whether by monetary policy or even by macroeconomic policy, unless you have some degree of coordination. What's happening today is we have no mechanisms other than summit meetings, which is rather inadequate, to deal with the fact that capital today is generally international. You have capital flights, capital movements of all kinds — not just capital moving but production units move. Labour does not move. But at the same time the problem is you cannot begin to deal with these problems in the terms of 'should we have more welfare or less welfare?,' or 'how do we pay for the welfare?,' if the structure within which you're talking is an antiquated structure and is not responsive to the new scales on which the economic activity is taking place. My fundamental argument would be until you have a matching political structure for the matching economic power, no particular set of policies will be effective. But that, it seems me, becomes a crucial problem. How do you have an understanding of the change of scale necessary for the new ways in which economic activity is taking place?

Ignatieff: Ulrich, can you comment on this?

Briefs: Well, if one tries to see the enormous and increasing structural contradictions which are inherent to our economic system, one very quickly gets the impression which was conveyed to us by Daniel Bell, that in a way our given political system, so to speak, is not able to cope with this. This is also my impression.

Rothschild: I think this is something that's said quite often now without people really thinking about the implications. Now, perhaps all that is meant is that one disagrees with the choice of political parties at the last election. And if that's all that's meant, well I mean, speaking of this country, the UK, which is my country, I disagree very much. But I think if one's saying something more fundamental than that, then it really is a rather dangerous thing to say. I mean, I certainly agree that the very high and continuing levels of unemployment pose very serious political dangers. And I certainly think that the pressure for continuing decline in real wages which is coming from several Western European governments now is also posing serious political questions. But is it really our political system that's at risk? I mean, the Swedish economist, Arthur Linbeck, who Professor Bell mentioned, says that there's a mismatch between political institutions and our economic needs. And I think that's not the kind of concern that should be bandied around very lightly without thinking about whether we really want to change basic democratic structures, for example.

Bell: Well, let's see if we can qualify the terms. I don't think anybody wants to attack in any way the notion of a democratic process and the rights of people to be able to control and have a say in what's going on. If I say that I think there is a mismatch of powers, it's the ability of a government to be effective. And I think to a large extent the nature of the changes in the international economy limits increasingly the effectiveness of governments in being able to do certain kinds of things. So that the internationalisation of capital is a limit. The whole question of control of one's own money supply is a limit. The flow of capital into different markets because of different interest rates, therefore limiting the ability of governments to finance certain things. For example, the Swedish government had a problem only recently, because when they were trying to finance some of the enterprises they were trying to do with selling of bonds, they couldn't attract enough money because capital was flowing out toward the United States. Therefore, I think there are some very real questions, and that's why I said the real problem was effective coordination of national systems.

Rothschild: But that's not the same as changing the political system.

Bell: No, I'm talking about national systems. The word political here, I think, has got us bogged down. I'm talking about the structure and size of a national state. And the ability of a national state to have control over activities within its borders and those who control it outside. And therefore, unless one can match political and economic power on the scale in which it works any political state, or any national state, would become increasingly ineffective. That's the argument I was making.

Ignatieff: What exactly did you mean, Ulrich, so that we clear up potential misunderstandings?

Briefs: Yeah, I think I should elaborate a bit upon this. I didn't plead for a deliberate change of the existing political system in every sense. I mean, I think that there are some needs that we have to envisage, certain very fundamental changes also for a political system, as a personal opinion.

Rothschild: But what sort of changes?

Briefs: We, the trade unions, for instance, in West Germany will always be among those who defend the existing democratic system. No doubt about this. But I was arguing the other way around. What was the experience from the twenties and the thirties in Germany, in Italy, in Japan, in a certain number of other countries? I mean, the attempts to change the essential basic features of our political systems will come from another way.

Bell: From the Right.

Briefs: From the Right. Let me quote one of the famous Russian statesmen of the first half of this century, who himself did not live through the crisis of the late twenties, early thirties. He once said 'the bourgeoisie doesn't know any economic situation without issue', meaning without a way out. Meaning if there is no economic way out they will have to look for a political way out. And that was what was operated in a certain number of countries towards the end of the twenties, respectively in the thirties. That is what I am afraid of. The Federal Republic, with all its traditions — and you must not forget that we have never gone through a real process of denazification — I wouldn't say that Hitler or the nazi regime would ever come again, that's not the point, but there are certain traditions which are in the minds of the population still to a large degree, and so on. We'll certainly not be the country which we are now if we have instead of an unemployment of 2.3 — in reality 4 million — which we have now, an unemployment in the realm of 6, 6.5 or 7 million. That is the danger.

Rothschild: But I think one ought to be proud of the way the political system has been working in Western Europe. I mean, if you compare what has happened in our countries to what's happened, for example, in Latin America, where there's been an industrial depression superimposed on existing levels of very acute deprivation in many countries without the institutions of the welfare state, well, things have really worked rather well from a political point of view.

Briefs: Well, you can always say that it could be worse.

Rothschild: And we should be proud that there has been up till now a consensus about the basic institutions of the welfare state. Of course, I'm extremely concerned about the efforts in the UK and in other countries among some political parties to say we must dismantle it in a wholesale way, but the misery that people have experienced, both economic and political and social, in the very serious economic crisis of the last ten years has not been anything like as bad as it was in the 1930s, and that's a resilience of political institutions as well as economic institutions.

Ignatieff: But isn't there another issue here? Which is, on the one hand there's the risk that if political systems over the next ten years are unable to answer or deal with the crisis of unemployment, there is the risk on the one hand of a return to authoritarian solutions. That's one kind of danger. But there's another kind of danger on the other side. That is, if you have a constantly changing economy, which is recombining the economy, throwing people out of work, creating new jobs, it seems to me one of the other risks is that you have a polity which doesn't give any impression that it controls the evolution of the economic system. I mean, what ultimately comes to be at stake, it seems to me, is the issue of sovereignty. That is, you have polities which over a long period of time simply fail to deliver on their essential promise. Which is that we ought to be masters in our own house. And it seems to me that's a quite strong risk.

Bell: Can I mediate the question this way? If one looks back at the twenties and thirties, there were four situations which conjoined to create the problems. One was a seemingly insoluble problem, which nobody knew how to deal with, which was unemployment. Even in the UK, you found people, for example, at the time of Tom Jones, who was the Secretary of the Cabinet, who wrote in his diary, and he was on the unemployment board, 'we have no way of knowing how to deal with the unemployment problem.' So you had a seemingly insoluble problem. You had a parliamentary system with no ability to control and to have an effective majority, and therefore the whole shifting coalitions and a high degree of inability to govern. You had, thirdly, private violence which the state couldn't control: the blackshirts, the brownshirts and various others. And fourthly, you had the disaffection of the intelligentsia. And you think of those four elements conjoining, and therefore you had the collapse in Portugal and Spain and Austria and almost in France and Germany etc. Now, I think Emma's certainly right that the political systems today are very different from that of the twenties and thirties and they have shown enormous resilience in this way. Private violence has been replaced by terrorism, which creates a certain degree of instability and fears and therefore creates a certain degree of retreat. The intelligentsia, I think, today, except in the UK, are no longer Left. I think it's quite striking throughout Western Europe

the intelligentsia has in effect, I think, been baffled by events and
don't know, in a sense, what to say. In the UK you still have a Left
intelligentsia which repeats old tired slogans, and that's a different
problem. But there is, it seems to me, to come back to the first one,
there's a growing sense of not knowing how to manage. For a while
it was inflation. People were worried — we forget this — people
were worried, and particularly in Germany, one of the fears of
reflation is the fact that you would have inflation. For ten or so
years, in the UK and in the United States government policy was
deliberately aimed to increase unemployment as a way of reducing
inflation. And you had of course the shrinkage of a large part of the
industrial base of this country in a very sharp recession in '80-81,
long before the American recession, to shrink the industrial base of
this country in order to wring out over-manning in this respect.
Monetary solutions have not been very effective. There is
increasingly some sense of dismay, and we may not just muddle
through. Then on top of that, you have the wholesale dislocations
which come from a new international division of labour, the
competition from the orient and the technological changes which
we're not managing very well. And what troubles me, and I think
Emma's perfectly right about the political resilience, what troubles
me is the lack of clarity of any kind about how to manage the
difficulties of unemployment and the trade-off versus inflation, the
whole question of transitions regarding jobs and, third, the new
international division of labour.

Ignatieff: I think that's where we should end. We began by talking
about technology, and I think one of the things that it's most
tempting to do with technology is to think of it as a kind of fate,
prescribing a fate that we can't evade or avoid. I think one of the
things this discussion has shown is that the problem is not
technology but politics and political will. And this discussion has
thrown up a dozen ways in which we can make the future different, a
dozen ways in which we can shape the future as we will. I think the
one problem that came up that seems to me to be very troubling is
that the economic space in which these changes occur is global. But
the political space remains the nation. We simply do not have
political instruments to master global economic change.

CHAPTER 5

The New Politics

Michael Ignatieff
with Ralph Dahrendorf and Alain Touraine

Ignatieff: In our last programme we wondered whether the modern age is giving way to a quite different kind of future, and we discovered it's already here. We tried to imagine how the new technology would transform not only work and the economy in our children's time, but what kind of society this might be. We found out how much microelectronics and automation have already transformed our own time. In this programme we want to look ahead at the politics of this new post-industrial society. That future too is already with us. An old politics of class, party and trade unions may be dying, but a new politics of sexual liberation, racial equality and ecology is still struggling to be born. Suddenly we're at a crossroads, uncertain where the signs are pointing. Are we living through the final hours of the working class movements of Europe? And if so, what kinds of movements could succeed them? What are the new issues, the new sites of struggle in the politics of this post-industrial future which is bearing down upon us?

To sharpen our focus on these questions, I have with me two of the first Europeans to identify these changes: Ralf Dahrendorf, former head of the London School of Economics and prominent liberal politician in Germany, and Alain Touraine, Professor at the Ecole des Hautes Etudes in Paris and a pioneer in the study of labour movements and their successors. Gentlemen, I thought we should try to begin by putting some signposts at that crossroads. And I'm just wondering, beginning with you, Ralf Dahrendorf, what you think are the changes in the post-industrial economy which is emerging that are going to transform the political agenda in the next decade?

Dahrendorf: Well, as you hinted in your initial remarks, I think many of these changes have happened already. The politics of our societies, and I'm talking about European countries in general, but also about the United States, Canada and comparable ones, is strangely frozen. That is to say, we've still got the same parties, they're still playing the same games, but somehow these games are no longer relevant to new issues. That I would indeed say. And so what appears to be the same is in fact almost an alienated superstructure over a totally different world. The real question is where do the new forces come from? What is it in our society that's new? And that's a big one. Just to give you a quick answer, I think there is a new social problem which we cannot easily deal with by the traditional measures of social policy, which is the new unemployment — or differently, the new poverty — and no doubt we'll get round to that. And there are various attempts to explore new ways of life, ranging from what I would call the technological fantasy, to the alternative lifestyle dreams.

Ignatieff: Why fantasy?

Dahrendorf: Oh, because I am not one of those who believes that technology is going to transform our lives totally, because it seems to me it's as much an instrument as it is a force of change — but perhaps we'll get to that too as we talk. No, you see, one of the characteristic features of thinking about politics in these last decades has been this search for the new. Where does the new come from? Now, the existing parties and party systems have been unprepared to absorb the new, because they've felt quite happy settling down in what I sometimes call the 'social democratic consensus' or the 'consensus of the majority class'. And those of us who've been looking for the new have been — I, at any rate — have been not overly enthusiastic with the signs of the new which we have discovered so far. So that's the kind of position which I see.

Ignatieff: Okay, the new. We've got unemployment, new kinds of employment. We've got a new kind of poverty. We've got new forms of technology. What else do we have to put on the agenda? (to Touraine) Do you agree with this diagnosis?

Touraine: I think the main characteristic of our society is that it is able to produce and transform not only material goods but symbolic goods: languages, information, images and so on. So that the main political problem moves from the economic sphere to the cultural one. And after all, the main problem is how is it possible to struggle against a cultural power which has a monopoly of the production and diffusion of information and images? That's why so many movements are geared toward creating alternative cultural expression. Even sometimes a new language. An American friend of mine was telling me a few days ago that after one year out of his university in the United States, when he comes back he doesn't understand people, because so many new words have been created. So I would say that now language, mass media, all kinds of cultural expression, are the places where interests oppose each other and where the main stakes of our political life stay. That is true in the sense of, for example, the situation of women. After all, it's true that the organised women's lib is not as strong as it used to be, but if you observe attitudes, custom, ideas, behaviour, you see that a tremendous transformation is created. So I would say this is one first point. That the main field of political problem is —

Ignatieff: Is symbolic action.

Touraine: — culture. Now, the second point — that's why I was mentioning women — is that we are interested in individuality and difference. We have no more social aims. I mean, in some sense our social movements are anti-social movements. Who is interested in creating a good society? All movements are trying to oppose society. Even when we say democracy, what was democracy in our European tradition? It means the sovereignty of the people. And now I would say that nobody would define democracy as the rule of the majority but as the respect of the minorities. And in the same sense what we called democracy is the absence of the sovereign, even the people, because we know what a popular democracy is, or what a people's democracy is.

Ignatieff: Ralf Dahrendorf, come in here.

Dahrendorf: I agree with your analysis to some extent, but not with the tone in which you couch it. I mean, I would go a step further than you. Because one of the interesting phenomena is that whereas in the past you could assume that those who were out actually aspired to be in, wanted to be in, today it is probably true to say that some of those who are just above the boundary line are more attracted by the new cultural developments below the boundary line than they are by the world in which they are living. So in fact it is true that certain new radiant centres of cultural orientation are emerging in groups which are economically, in the old terms, highly disadvantaged and socially defined out. Fair enough. But this doesn't solve the economic and social problem. And there is still the tremendous issue of how you create a society — you would say a nation, and I would accept that because I think nation and citizenship are very closely related — how you create a society where everybody belongs. Now you might argue that by an infusion of certain new values into total society, that is by the alliance between innovators and some of the poor, you might bring this about. What I see at the moment is something quite different. I see these traces, and I think they're quite rudimentary, of new cultures, with their attractiveness for some of those who are in, as essentially a fundamental questioning of the social contract. I believe that what we're experiencing today is a questioning of the contract on which citizenship and the nation and our societies are themselves based, and I am greatly impressed, which I don't say lightly as a liberal, by issues of law and order. That is to say, by issues of the validity of certain general norms and the acceptance of certain rules by which we all abide, and by the extent to which what I call impunity, that is the unreadiness to apply sanction, or inability to apply sanctions to certain groups, dominates our lives. So, while I think that there is a lot of truth to your analysis, I think it does not imply an answer. It does not imply a solution. It only aggravates the problem.

Touraine: I said a moment ago that in the past we always thought that the end of politics was to help create a good society. That means that we were accustomed to think that social problems and political problems and state problems are directly connected together. The best expression of that is the concept of revolution, which dominated the Western world from the French revolution to the Chinese one, passing through the Russian one. This identification of social and political categories, we no longer think that way. Why? Because we are not living in a state which is the *état de droit*, in the old British and French tradition. Because our state is now an entrepreneur. Our state is not at the centre, it is at the frontier struggling in an international competition. And social problems are less political problems because they are more cultural. So now there's a huge distance between state problems and social problems. That's the newest expression of this new social movement, that there are currents of opinion and they don't care about power. And so what happens to the go-betweens? I mean, to political parties? What I observe is that we are living after a long period of all politics, a kind of Sartrean period if you like, or a Thomas Mann period as well, for half a century. Now, on the contrary, politics is low profile and there are no longer any political passions in Europe. And that has good aspects. Using a German word, the compensation for this lower level of political life is a wider and higher importance of *öffentlichkeit*.

Ignatieff: Which means?

Touraine: Public opinion, the public space. And nobody is quite conscious of this fact, including, I would say Habermas himself, who has a much too pessimistic view about what happens to this public space. We are living in a period of tremendous development of public opinion, including through mass media which are supposed to manipulate — and that is not true. So, politics is uninteresting. Public opinion is lively. And social movements, social actors and intellectuals, want to express themselves at the public opinion level, not at the political level and even less at the state level. And that is the growing differentiation, which transforms the whole political problem.

Ignatieff: (to Dahrendorf) What do you make of that account of what's happening?

Dahrendorf: Well, here we have a slight problem of language. I don't disagree with what Alain Touraine says but I'm not sure I would express it in these terms. You see, the question which I ask myself, as he does, is where do the new forces come from? And like you, I feel we should not look for traditional answers to that because they are not likely to be in the traditional field. Let me give you one example, and then see whether we agree on that. I remember in the 1960s Ken Galbraith introduced the notion that we're simultaneously having private wealth and public squalor. Now that was a relatively simple one and a lot was done in the 1960s and one of the themes of the 1960s was the strengthening of the state in the sense in which Touraine has just described it. But then came another thesis, which I think is quite interesting, which is that all our lives, in all our lives, we experience — and I'm now talking about the large middle class, which incidentally we mustn't forget in our analysis because they still have problems and they are most of the voters — we have certain areas in which we are relatively well off or at any rate in which we can hope to satisfy the aspirations of our lives within the existing framework. And we have other areas in which, in a sense, we are all underprivileged, however rich we are.

Ignatieff: And those are?

Dahrendorf: For instance, the environment. It's a very interesting one, the whole environmental area. It's not one which mobilises a new group. That's an error, to believe that there can be a new group which can be mobilised simply because it's something which affects absolutely everybody. And so it is quite right to talk about the disparity of certain sectors of life, whereas in some sectors we're relatively well provided, in other sectors we all suffer. And these other sectors can become quite virulent from time to time. So I would agree that the nature of politics is quite different. That it is more situational. And if one accepts that, then it is actually true that there is a public which is quite effective, because this situational public, citizens' initiatives —

Ignatieff: What do you mean by situational?

Dahrendorf: I mean by that that these people are not organised in huge organisations which exist forever but they emerge in —

Ignatieff: Issue by issue.

Dahrendorf: — certain situations. Issue by issue is too narrow a view. It's the American view of what happens.

Ignatieff: Situation by situation.

Dahrendorf: I'm not really talking about the local road, I'm talking about fairly important areas which could even include things like human relations in industry or something of this kind. But areas of life rather than overriding interests which assemble groups of people. And around these areas of life you get from time to time quite virulent activity, quite important activity, and quite public activity and effective activity, actually, and that's where the media and many other factors come in.

Ignatieff: Where are your disagreements with Touraine? There's something about the tone of what Touraine is saying which is bothering you.

Touraine: Yes, but excuse me, before we disagree I would like to say just one word, say how much I agree with what Ralf Dahrendorf says. Because one of the most important transformations in political life is that people below, people who are supposed to be actors of a certain kind of protest, do not oppose particular interests. I mean, serfs or slaves could oppose the owner or the landowner of themselves, or even the worker in his factory was attacking the owner of the factory. The worker against manager, if you like. And now the new fact is that, as Dahrendorf rightly says, the power is applied to transform the whole of the environment, the whole of the public space — let's say nuclear policy or hospitals or education or mass media. And Dahrendorf used a word I considered the best to define the new actor, the *public*. It's not a class, it's not a group, it's not an interest group, a category, a stratum, it's the *public*. And the new problem there for social scientists is to understand how a public and not a specific group can act, can become *für sich*. Before it was relatively simple. And now it's more difficult. Maybe I would disagree on the point that I don't see why this public should not be able to become active as former workers or peasants or anybody you like. But the channels are different, and that's why public opinion channels, mass media, intellectuals play an absolutely central role.

Ignatieff: Look, one of the things that I'm missing when I listen to both of you is we've got a sense of an emerging social actor called the public. We've got a sense also of an underclass. What I miss in this analysis is who the enemy is. That is one of the cleverest things, I think, that Alain Touraine has said in the past is the argument that a social movement's success depends on the precision with which it identifies its antagonist. So who's the antagonist in the politics of tomorrow? The workers' movement of the past had capital and capitalists as its antagonist. Who's the opponent now? The corporate middle class with their privileges? The technocracy? Capital? The State? What's missing in this analysis is what has to be changed and where are the sources of resistance? Ralf Dahrendorf, do you have any thoughts on it?

Dahrendorf: Well, I don't have to find the enemy because it's not my theory which you're talking about.

Ignatieff: Well, could you try living within the theory for a minute?

Dahrendorf: I think Alain Touraine has actually answered the question just a moment ago when he himself talked about the simpler world in which one could identify the enemy. I believe the enemy, and this is quite serious, is in the rigidities of a system which turns protective and is unwilling to entertain the impulses which the public might try to feed into it. And these rigidities cannot be identified with simple individuals. People try, you see, and their favourite bogeymen, bureaucracy is one of them, the unions are another one, the state sometimes is. And it is true that all these institutions contribute in their own way to rigidities. At least, some of them do and to some extent they do. But I don't think it's possible to identify those who are in them as the enemy, because they are at the same time members of the public which is demanding change. So in an odd way we are actually talking about a system, and perhaps that's harder to combat than an enemy whom you can name. At least that's my own feeling.

Ignatieff: But doesn't that view, just to pursue it, simply negate the inbuilt structural inequalities of privilege? That is to say that the system is simply to evade identifying where it is that change has to occur specifically?

Dahrendorf: I can say where change has to happen specifically. That's not the problem. What is difficult in our society is not only to say who prevents it, but also how one actually goes about implementing the changes which one has in mind. Incidentally, all the time I am not overlooking how much still remains to be done within the old framework. Let's just put this on one side. We're talking here about whatever you want to call it.

Ignatieff: The future.

Dahrendorf: The future and the place of modernity. There's still a great deal to do in the old terms and there's still a great deal of reality to the old conflicts, but we neglect that for the moment. Also, I'm not one of those who minimise problems by neutralising the enemy. That is, by just saying 'the system' and there it is and you can't do anything about it. But I am convinced that all of us, in some of our capacities, prevent change and that all of us, in some of our capacities, need and want change. And if we continue to give in to the former impulse I think the danger is very great that we will create a kind of rigidity in which there will be a demand for unreasonable gods who are brought out from some machine. That is to say, the old risk of fascism, in my view, is not dead and has a great deal to do with the questions which you are now asking, namely where does all this come from? How does one bring about change in a situation in which one doesn't have an identifiable enemy and in which it's not simply a question of removing a few people or forcing a few people to give way? I think you won't get a much more precise answer, you will get a great deal of concern about rigidity and innovation.

Touraine: Well, here I feel like following a different path. I acknowledge that this problem of rigidity is very important. But I think it's possible to define, not — I don't like the expression 'the enemy' because it doesn't help building an analysis — but where power is. Let's take a very concrete and very fundamental example, and I will choose it precisely because it has obviously no negative connotation. We can speak of a medical power, because what we know about our body, our health, our life, our death, has been created by hospitals. And obviously I'm not going to say this is a technocracy full stop. No, medicine, during the last 30 or 40 years, has been able to create a representation of human beings like, after all, what we know about the whole world is created, shaped by television. And what do we observe? We observe, at a very low level, that this growing separation between illness and medicine on one side and individuals on the other side creates a kind of anti-medicine, so-called 'natural' medicine, very often at an extremely low level. But these people are trying to break medicine like Luddites, workers in Lancashire, were trying to break the first machines or the Canut in Lyons in 1831. But that indicates a problem. That doesn't mean that doctors are bad. That would be ridiculous. That means that there is a very central problem.

Ignatieff: But it's a site of social change.

Touraine: So, we already observe that is typically public, because there is no specific group which goes to the hospital, everybody does. But we, all of us, consider that this is one of the major problems, an ethical, cultural and then social and political problem. Now, what can we do about fecundation, about the management of death? Or about the management of sexuality and reproduction? These are major problems. I would observe in my own country that when we nationalise banks and big industry, nobody moves. Now if there is some rumour that the government is going to transform television, or that doctors are creating artificial fecundation, it's absurd, I mean, everybody is really interested and participative. I said a moment ago there are no more political passions, but there are ethical and cultural and then social passions. This is a new problem.

Dahrendorf: But then you would have to argue that the enemy — and I'm going to take the word because it's quite a handy one in this connection — that the enemy is actually the political class. Because if you look at politics, one is struck by one thing above all, and that is how it is virtually impossible to change things in any significant sense from traditional positions of power. That is, the changes which you have talked about are cultural changes which then spread through society and have a major influence on people's lives but which are not brought about by those who are the traditional incumbents of positions of power. And those who are the traditional incumbents of positions of power, if they have certain views of what should be different, very often feel that by having a position of power they're prevented from doing what they want to do. So if innovation, in your view, has to come from the cultural or the symbolic or the representational sphere, then you would have to argue, I believe, that the real obstacle, to use a more careful word, the real obstacle is in official politics and now what you want to fight is the official political system.

Touraine: You see, I would agree with your word 'obstacle', which is not the same thing. And just to indicate how these cultural problems have very concrete economic consequences, I would insist on the fact that today, I think, in all Western countries, if you are trying to identify new demands which can develop themselves in a situation of a higher productivity, I would say the major demand in our society is individualisation of services. And probably more in health than in education, and in education than free time activities.

Ignatieff: What do you mean exactly by individualisation of services? I don't follow.

Touraine: I mean that people who are submitted to hospital life, to mass medicine, want to be attended more individually. Not just because it's better, because they want illness not too separated from their situation as patients. Exactly like a worker doesn't want his work to be alienated, if I may use that word, from his personality. And now there is a debate, which is a very open one, and that's why the expression 'enemy' is very dangerous. Because we need a development of the medical system. We need a development of mass media. We need a development of research and development and information processing and so on, and the capacity of artificial intelligence. We need all of that.

Dahrendorf: But we won't have it.

Touraine: We can have it.

Dahrendorf: Well, will not. Our great middle class will tinker and tinker and tinker with the existing system and it'll become more and more absurd, but it won't be changed.

Ignatieff: Why are you so sure?

Dahrendorf: Because I'm convinced of these rigidities which are brought to bear on those who take decisions.

Touraine: I would agree with you. I would agree with you. But adding one thing which is essential for me: that it's not enough to say the middle class, the middle group, will oppose change. I think the main problem is to understand new problems, new conflict, and to reconstruct social actors. This middle — you cannot say this middle group — central group, will win, will resist. It will resist if new actors are not built, and if they are built the whole situation will be transformed. And I think in many ways the political situation is already transformed in a superficial, in a partial way, is already transformed by these new problems. And more negatively, you were quite right in observing that there is no motivation — social, cultural motivation — behind political forces. And you said, quite rightly and even more centrally, the ambiguity of the situation is that this public is at the same time this middle group. And that, I would say, in each of us, not just of them, is a contradiction, which after all is a little bit similar to what we knew in the past century where everybody, or a large part of the people, were citizens and even workers but at the same time were the middle class in terms of people who had received rights after the French Revolution, so we were conservative and progressive at the same time. But the whole political process will be open for that very reason, and the political situation will be transformed if we can reorganise new actors. Let's take an example that I mentioned a moment ago, the women's movement. Weak political actor, but look at the tremendous cultural and social transformations which have been introduced. And why? Not because they were fighting for equality, which is a very limited goal, but because women's lib deeply transformed our concept of the self, of the ego, of the subject, I would say.

Dahrendorf: Let me argue a slightly contrary case. The women's movement, I would say, is the tail end of the historical development of citizenship. And it is part and parcel of a movement in which universal suffrage has its place and many many other developments have their place. What is characteristic of our own time is that the large middle group as we've called it here, what I sometimes call the majority class, with an impermissable use of the word class, but still I call it that sometimes, is becoming frightened. And as it becomes frightened and protective it is in fact less able to live with difference than one would have hoped.

Touraine: Oh quite right.

Dahrendorf: And perhaps to some extent even less than at a time at which people were more confident, were looking forward to a better future and trusting their strength more.

Touraine: That could feed a new Bonapartism.

Dahrendorf: Yes, I mean suddenly some of the differences which we are faced with in our societies seem to become more disruptive, more liable to lead to quasi-civil wars. If anything, it is more difficult today to defend immigrants or to defend people of a different colour or whatever, people who are different. And all that is the consequence of a fearful and, for that reason, protective and inward-looking majority class and not of the great new future which you are describing.

Ignatieff: I want to get to this question — just before we move on — this question of fear. I think you've put your finger on something important. Let's talk about the fear. What's it a fear of? Where's it coming from?

Dahrendorf: Oh, that one may not be able to maintain the position one has. It's a very simple fear that you've got certain things or certain prospects perhaps and there are lots of things which threaten these prospects, lots and lots. And so, you know, they start in trade and go all the way to these cultural phenomena which we have talked about.

Ignatieff: But I get a feeling — just let me try to understand where you disagree — I mean, I hear you talking the language of a politics of long-term secular decline, which produces fear. I hear you, on the other hand, speaking a rather different language, that is the politics of the future will be a politics of change which forces actors to change no matter how devoted they are to their rigidities. Whereas I hear you saying we're in a long-term declining situation where those rigidities can only grow worse because the pie slowly shrinks.

Touraine: Maybe there is no disagreement actually, on that point. Because I think these are two phenomena, as I said at the beginning, new social problems, new social actors *and* a transformation of the international scene. We are no longer assured of controlling our environment in its changes. So at that first level I would entirely agree with Dahrendorf in saying that we are living, despite what so many people say, in a situation of decreasing tolerance. Because after all, a society like, let's say, Britain in the 19th century, which was so secure about itself, is a very open society. And we, all of us, in Europe in some sense were extremely open societies. And now it's true that we are living in a petit bourgeois world which is insecure and which is very ready to exclude a lot of minorities. Now, that is one side of the problem, or one type of problem. The other one is that nevertheless our societies are transforming themselves and they have internal problems. Now, I would agree one more fact, just to add to Dahrendorf's pessimism, and it is that this capacity for exclusion of our societies doesn't come only from an international situation but the fact that the social problems today deal with cultural values. It's much more difficult to accept a discussion about values than a discussion about interests. So we are in a less and less secularised society. We are no longer in a Weberian society. And now what is the main problem today at the world level? Islam is.

Dahrendorf: Fundamentalists. Turning away from a particular system.

Touraine: So there is, to use the traditional German opposition between society and community: *Gesellschaft* and *Gemeinschaft*, there is a kind of wider *Gemeinschaften*.

Ignatieff: What do you mean by that?

Touraine: I mean, people want to go back, a returnism and —

Dahrendorf: Re-communitarisation — how's that? (laughs). Sorry, terrible word.

Touraine: Neo-communitarian movements are present all over the world, you see. And that, I think, not only has nothing to do with these new social actors I was mentioning but is exactly the contrary.

Ignatieff: Why the contrary? Spell that out.

Touraine: Again, let's go back to the past for a while. What we have learned is that even in, let's say, the labour movement, or even in a movement towards citizenship like the French Revolution, there is what I would call an anti-movement. The terror, for the political movement — obviously Stalinism or Leninism for the labour movement — and now in these new social movements which want to develop a sense of identity, difference, communication and so on, there is always present an anti-movement which is recreating communities, ghettos and excluding minorities or innovators, which is to a certain extent the same thing. So, our social movements are more fragile. And after all, you see, the situation is that in the past we had a very limited, very important, but very strong movement. In a certain sense even the workers, the peasants in the past, even the slaves in the past, were able to revolt. But very limited. I mean the public space, the political space was extremely limited. Now, it's wide open but fragile. And it's very difficult to transform these demands, passions and so on into a continuous and organised action. It's a new type of difficulty. But what I wanted to make clear in this discussion with Ralf Dahrendorf is that we should analyse the problems of the formation of new social actors and then, if I may speak that way, consider the resistances. And I would agree that we are in a situation where quite likely the resistances to innovation and conflict are growing. And that is a very real danger.

Ignatieff: Now one of the curious things that's happened in this discussion is that a word has been missing throughout, a word has just vanished from the discussion. And that's the word 'socialism'. A lot of people listening to you will listen with a certain kind of outrage, a sense that this is the word, this is the movement, this is the ideology which has been the bearer of our firmest and deepest hopes, ethical hopes, social hopes, political hopes. Why is it that that word has dropped out of your vocabulary? Specifically, why do you think that socialism as an ideology, socialism as a movement, can no longer be that new social movement, that bearer of change, that focuser of hope in the years to come? Ralf Dahrendorf.

Dahrendorf: You know, it's anybody's guess what name innovation will have in different countries, and I can imagine all sorts of names for what's going to happen. My own view about socialism, for what it's worth — and can I say in parenthesis I think it's been a quality of this particular discussion that it didn't occur to us to introduce the going phrases for things, but instead we talked about things — but my own understanding is that there are three basic meanings of socialism today. And I can comment on each of them in one sentence. One is the traditional socialism of social democrats in the European continental sense, which has gone into the society in which we're living and which determines the society in which we're living; one is the notion that the problems we have are all due to the fact that we haven't done enough of all this and that we have to go much further along this line — I personally believe that that is not very interesting advice — and then there is a new school of thinking, which is probably quite closely related to some of the values which we were talking about earlier, which sees socialism connected with new values, work and environment for example, connected with a greater role of every citizen in the determination of affairs, democratisation and all that. And that I think we have discussed to some extent although we haven't given it a name.

Ignatieff: Alain Touraine.

Touraine: Well, obviously a lot of people who call themselves socialist can defend very many different ideas. Nevertheless, I think it's necessary to indicate that the history of socialism came to a close. What is socialism? It's the ideology of the labour movement. And the labour movement said 'I'm struggling against management, I'm not able to create a new society. The creation of a new society must be made through a naturalisation of society through the state, through science, intellectuals and the state.' And now new social movements, new social actors don't think that way. They don't think that there is a level, an inferior level for social movement and an upper level for political and state action. On the contrary, as I said before, these movements want to be organised by themselves even if they are quite weak. And in a sense then they oppose themselves to the state. So the whole union between protest, social protest and state, which is the real definition of socialism, is now out of our present time. And what we observe is that in all countries, including in social democratic countries — let's take an example of Sweden, as a major social democratic country — we are the first generation in which social democracy represented all, that is the labour movement. And in the new generation it's basically a consensor state. It's an integration of society, the development, the hyper-development of this majority class through the state. And so I would say socialism from that point of view is no longer carrying new motivation and forces for social transformation. That does mean that a lot of people who call themselves socialist are not active agents of social and cultural transformation. But I think it's necessary after all, it's necessary to make a break like people in the last century did. The ideas of the French Revolution were progressive and yet these republicans finally shot the first organised workers. And in the world today, because we are not speaking just about Europe, the word socialist describes tanks more often than strikes.

Ignatieff: Okay, but that's in Eastern Europe.

Touraine: Not always Eastern Europe, part of Asia, many parts of the world.

Ignatieff: Okay, a significant portion of the world, I won't deny.

Touraine: In spite of our vocabulary.

Ignatieff: But in this world, the world that we're talking about, most of the important social struggles of the last 10 to 15 years have actually been carried out by people calling themselves socialists.

Touraine: I would disagree with that.

Dahrendorf: I would disagree with that too.

Ignatieff: Why?

Dahrendorf: I can't think of a single important political struggle of the last 10-15 years.

Ignatieff: The miners' strike?

Touraine: No.

Dahrendorf: You think that's an important political struggle of the last 10 or 15 years?

Touraine: No, not at all.

Ignatieff: But it's here.

Touraine: No, Let's not confuse two things. One is struggles, conflict, which have a social or political weight. They matter. And another thing is a conflict, or attitude or opinion which carries a new kind of protest and demand which transform the political and social scene. And if you consider most European states, I would say that women, ecologists, the sixties student movement and others —

Ignatieff: Were not socialist?

Touraine: No, what I would say is they feel linked with a socialist tradition, like socialism felt linked with a republican tradition.

Dahrendorf: Right.

Touraine: A lot of people said let's stop this reference to 'bourgeois democracy', and they wanted to emphasise the opposition between social problems and purely institutional problems. I think we have exactly the same necessity today, to indicate clearly that there is a discontinuity between social problems and conflict which are based on working conditions and problems and conflict which are based on the manipulation of culture.

Ignatieff: A final question, gentlemen. I'm always thinking of my children, what's going to be the dominant political issue for my children, 20 years from now?

Dahrendorf: In 20 years time I think the system in which we're going to live will not have changed an awful lot. There will still be a fairly strange continuation of a traditional party game, with some changes in some countries and yet no major change with respect to the things we have talked about. And there will still be the social developments outside the party system. I think the lingering crisis of legitimacy will go on for quite a long time.

Ignatieff: Alain Touraine.

Touraine: Well, my answer would be the same and different at the same time. I think changes not only will occur but they already have occurred. We would not have spoken the same way five or ten years ago. Because, I mean, the decline of political definitions and interest has been extremely rapid. And what I think is that, in 20 years from now, we'll be in a more and more fragile situation, in the sense that on the one side modernisation of social and political life will have developed itself, and on the other side the constraints and limitation will have increased, partly for demographic reasons. I mean, the weight of the minimum social integration will be much more heavy to carry than now. So the possibilities of innovation will decrease. And that should give some dramatic aspects to our discussion. If we don't solve our problem, if we don't transform our social and political life, it will be much more difficult to achieve such a transformation in 20 years from now. So we are probably living our last decades of nations with large endogenous capacity of transformation.

Ignatieff: Gentlemen, I think that's where we're going to leave it. What strikes me, I want to draw on one thing that was said by Ralf Dahrendorf earlier, which is that blaming someone else for resistance to change is an alibi. The real sources of resistance that are most difficult to confront are the ones within ourselves. We are all both proponents of change and also deeply conservative, deeply rooted to the old ways. The problem is us.

CHAPTER 6

Lost Illusions

Michael Ignatieff
with Octavio Paz and Leszek Kolakowski

Ignatieff: Our century has not been kind to hope, and it has been merciless towards utopia. Those who put their faith in art, science or revolution to change the world are older and wiser. The 19th century faith in science seems ironic now, in a century of total war and total pollution. The modernist utopias of art and architecture seem quaint and dated museum pieces. The political utopias of socialism and the revolutionary tradition lie buried somewhere in the mass graveyards of Stalinism and the cultural revolution. Too many heads have been broken in the name of too many Brave New Worlds. So the question, in an age of disillusion is what future for utopia? What future for hope itself? Two men have lived through the experiences of this history of disillusion, and they're with me tonight. Octavio Paz, the distinguished Mexican poet and author of *The Labyrinth of Solitude*, knew the surrealists in Paris, was involved in the Spanish civil war, and has been an important witness to the crisis of socialism. Leszek Kolakowski has taught the history of philosophy in Warsaw, Chicago and Oxford, where he is now a fellow of All Souls. His writings chronicle the crises of faith which have afflicted both Christianity and Marxism. I thought I'd begin with you, Professor Kolakowski, but it's a question to both of you in effect. In an earlier programme Saul Bellow used a very nice phrase, he talked about the 'formation of a soul', and I'm wondering whether both of you could talk about the formations of your souls, particularly your passage from the Marxism of your early youth to your modern position in which both of you are essentially critics of modern socialism. And could we start with you, Professor Kolakowski?

Kolakowski: Communism appeared to myself and to many people, attractive because it offered a kind of all-encompassing, all-explaining framework for thought which embraced both the entire past history and the hope for the future, and at the same time the awareness, the consciousness of being on the morally good side, on the side of the oppressed and poor and so on. And at the same time, I think we saw communism as a kind of continuation of Enlightenment, which it was in a way, it was a bastard offspring of the Enlightenment, and it preserved in caricature form something of it. Well, obviously these illusions step by step were dispersed. It turned out — you might say it is not a surprising discovery — but eventually it turned out that if you rule with terror you are left with terror, instead of using terror for the sake of freedom and general happiness. What was really the most annoying, the most depressing, and the most horrifying in communism, was, I would say, less terror, less oppression and exploitation — but felt especially strongly of course by intellectuals — was the universal lie. Really, communism is a kingdom of lies. The lie is all-pervading. Everything is poisoned with lies. So the spiritual liberation is perhaps the most important aspect of the mental liberation from all this stuff.

Ignatieff: Is the liberation from the lie?

Kolakowski: Yes.

Ignatieff: We have there one history of the soul. I'm wondering what story you can lay beside that one, Octavio Paz.

Paz: This is slightly different to the experience of Kolakowski of course. He's from Poland, he has been through communism. I have never been in a communist country. I have never lived in a communist country. And then I am not a philosopher, I am a poet, I am a writer. And I'm Mexican. I am from the outside of the Western world. Even if we Mexicans, we Latin Americans, we belong to the Western world, they say we are the Third World. You know it's a lie, it's not only a Marxist lie but a universal lie. Well, when I was young I also was very much near the communists. I was never a member of the communist party. And the reasons why I was so near the communists were more or less the same as Kolakowski. First, Marxism offers a total explanation of life, and also is a key of history, the key of the future. Then there is justice. It's a philosophy, an ideology which tries to identify itself with social justice and with the liberation not only of the working class but mankind. Then peace, it's a peaceful ideology. Then in the case of Mexico nationalism was very important. But not because we were fighting against nationalism as in Poland, but because we were fighting American imperialism. Marxism was very important because it was a way to fortify our nationalism. Finally, when I was young it was the period of the great growth of fascism and nazism in Germany. And then my youth coincided with the Spanish republic and we were on the side of the Spanish republic, and to defend the Spanish republic, we start to defend also the communist side, who were partisan of the Spanish republic of course, helping the republicans. But that's the political reasons. There are also deeper things perhaps. I was writing poetry, and my idea, the idea of my generation of poetry was slightly different from the idea of the former generation. For the former generation, the activity of being a poet was to write poems. For us, the important thing was not to write poems, but to change nature, to change life, to change mankind. In some way, for us, poetry was linked with magic, with religion, but of course with politics. It was a revolutionary force. Poetry was a way to change mankind, to change the nature of man. Poetry in some way as revelation of hidden realities, but also poetry as revolution, as a changing of reality, social realities, historical realities etc. Then the reality very soon disappointed me. For me, poetry should be a revolutionary force, and for them it was not that. From the beginning I was a paradox to my Marxist friends. In my evolution perhaps also was very important all the Stalinism, the Moscow process etc. I was living in Mexico. I witnessed the killing of Trotsky. It affected me very deeply. There were many political exiles in Mexico, like Victor Serge, the Marxist revolutionary, he was a friend of mine. I began to understand the real nature of Stalinism. Then in Paris I was a friend of the surrealists. Surrealists tried to be revolutionary but also non-Stalinist. It was a very difficult enterprise, but for me it was very important, all this. And then finally after so many years I decided first that poetry is not to change mankind, but for the revelation of mankind, is a work made of words, not of acts. That poetry is a vision, but also is a verbal object, a rhythmic object, that is not magic, that is art, is poetry. Secondly, that we should see revolutions in the modern times with critical eyes. Because revolutions are the daughters of aspiration, of freedom, but they are the mothers of despotism, modern despotism.

Ignatieff: Let me invoke in both of your cases the fact that you're both at the edges of the European world. That is, Poland is fully part of European culture but because of the Cold War and the iron curtain it is now a country apart in some sense. Mexico, you reject quite rightly the kind of label of the Third World, and you're a Mexican whose whole life has been imbued with European culture, but still both of you are men who are at the edges of this culture, which is the centre of our programme really. The sense that this culture is in crisis, Western European culture, I'm just wondering what that sense of being at the edge of it has done to your awareness of the dimensions of that crisis. That is, why is it that the apple, the fruit of Western modernisation, Western modernity, Western progress, seems so rotten to so many of the people who are eating the fruit or benefiting from it?

Kolakowski: Well I wish I knew exactly where the root of this disenchantment was, because it's not necessarily what people normally say about it. Of course, we know all of the possible disasters, possible war, pollution and overpopulation and so on, so there's no need to dwell on those destructive sides of modernity.

Everybody knows that. But I think that the disenchantment with modernity goes much deeper, whether or not it's expressed in this way. I think that at a certain moment in European history, in fact in the late Middle Ages, the old order had begun to crumble, I mean the cosmos in which all sides of human life and human activities had a well-defined place. Religion, philosophy, art and politics, were somehow part of a unified order voted by the divine wisdom. Now this order, this cosmos was gradually crumbling and this is precisely what modernity is about.

Ignatieff: The crumbling of that order?

Kolakowski: The crumbling of this order, the separation and autonomisation of various sides of human activity, or various forms of culture, the growth of rationalism. And communism, seen from this perspective, can be interpreted as a caricatural attempt to restore this unity by coercion and despotism. After all, art emancipated itself entirely in the Middle Ages and Renaissance. It has become an autonomous form of life and not necessarily an instrument at the service of other objectives. Communism for the first time tried to restore to art its edifying function. The result was of course destruction of art. To the extent that it fulfils the role which communism wants it to fulfil, art is destroyed. In other words, this order seems to us impossible to be revealed in another form but caricatural totalitarianism. But we feel of course, all of us I think, we feel we are in a kind of malaise precisely because this order has ultimately crumbled.

Ignatieff: Octavio Paz, how do you react to that account? That is, a disenchantment, a malaise that is rooted in the loss of an order that was sustained by religion?

Paz: Kolakowski is right. And it can be applied, this idea of the breaking of the old Christian order, not only to communism as a substitute, but also to fascism. After all, the great attraction that fascism had among some poets, English poets or American poets like Ezra Pound, or writers such as Claudel in France —

Kolakowski: Celine.

Paz: Yes, Celine. All of them were attracted because nazism and fascism also tried to substitute Christian order, but a new order founded in the idea of race, in the idea of the state, in the idea of old Rome and many other things. But also it was the idea of order. Now, it is true that we are in a terrible situation because the freedom that we are living has a double face. It's first the possibility to do things that we can do, but also it is not an answer to the most important problems for us. That is, Western civilisation, the state, economy. Philosophy doesn't answer, or answers only in a very limited way, the basic questions of mankind. And there appear the ghosts of religion. There is a kind of emptiness inside of each of us.

And this emptiness can be filled with caricatures such as communism or fascism or totalitarian ideas, or with sects, all this flowering of superstitious selfs in the Western world, or with authentic religion. But that is very difficult for us.

Kolakowski: Disenchantment with humanism and rationalism?

Paz: Yes.

Ignatieff: But let's put a hard question to that. A sceptic would say to you that both of your remarks have been premised on a non-historical idea. That is, that human beings have some immanent, permanent need for religious experience or for religious symbolisation, which if denied produces the malaise, produces the disenchantment.

Kolakowski: Why do you think it a-historical?

Ignatieff: Well, what I would say potentially is the idea that the historical, the contingent historical bearer of those needs was religion, but that doesn't mean that with religion's disappearance a vacuum or a void necessarily has to appear. Do you see what I mean? That is, there are millions of people, it seems to me, in the Western world who live the death of god, the disappearance of religion, with absolutely no consciousness whatsoever of a void or an emptiness.

Kolakowski: Obviously it is the case that people can survive and be decent persons without any attachment to religion. Of course it is possible. We are talking, however, of cultural processes on a large scale. I didn't say anything about instinct. What I mean is that so far historical experience seems to confirm this idea to the effect that the dying religions are replaced not by enlightened humanism but by the caricatures of religions. And it is the case that people feel that there is a very widely spread discomfort in those fruits of the Enlightenment. I'm not saying now how far it is justified but it is certainly the fact that it is discomfort, 'Civilisation and its Discomforts', which I think is the title of this series, which is the title, of course of Freud's famous essay.

Ignatieff: But Freud precisely regarded that set of religious instincts as a set of conditional historical illusions which, with the progress represented by the conquest of nature, the conquest of human fear in front of nature, would disappear. And so an analysis of modernity which says we are all filled with a kind of aching void left by the departure of the gods presumes that somehow the presence of the gods was always eternally a kind of human instinct. And I find that a sympathetic view but I find it philosophically a questionable one. That's my point.

Kolakowski: Let's leave aside Freud. It has been repeatedly pointed out that Freud's concept of human nature was essentially based on his contacts with upper middle class Viennese Jews whom he somehow took as a very representative sample of mankind. And I don't think he was consistent in his views on religion. I mean, what he says in *The Future of an Illusion* I don't think is consistent with his other writings which show religion as a kind of cure for the discontent in civilisation, at the same time pointing out that this discontent is bound to grow because there is no possible reconciliation of instincts with civilisation. But let's leave aside Freud. Nobody can say on the basis of any empirical evidence that there is an eternal or instinct or something implanted in us, this idea of god implanted in our minds, and which has been there from time immemorial, we do not know that. Perhaps it is so, perhaps it is not. The fact is simply that we witness an unprecedented collapse of religious tradition and I think we have good reasons to connect this collapse with so many negative phenomena, phenomena which are universally assessed as negative in our culture, and with this feeling of malaise. We don't need really to make for this purpose metaphysical assumptions.

Paz: Well I should say then two things about instinct. I was using this word with purpose and trying to put it as a universal need. When I was talking about need I was thinking of Hume, the idea that we experiment with need to find a genuine design, a general order in the cosmos. And that is very interesting because it comes from the 18th century.

Ignatieff: From the heart of scepticism in fact.

Paz: From the heart of scepticism. And that is very important in a dialogue that is a critique of religion. That is why it's so important. Then I think that our position facing religion is ambiguous because I feel that I am the descendant, the son of the Enlightenment, more than anything, but, being Mexican, I am also the son of the Counter Reformation, and that they are fighting in myself as I suppose in everybody. Perhaps you, being Polish, have another protagonist of the same dialogue inside you, but you have a dialogue, you are ambiguous facing religion in many aspects, I suppose. In my case I am ambiguous because religion in itself is ambiguous. You go on to religions, many beautiful things, we own Buddha, we own Christ, but we also own the Inquisition, religious wars, human sacrifices etc. And we own also caricatures of religion and all these totalitarian states.

Ignatieff: (to Kolakowski) Would you describe yourself as both a child of the Enlightenment and a child of the Counter Reformation?

Kolakowski: Yes. Yes, I think that a fitting description. And of course, as Octavio has just said, we are all ambiguous about it. Because we see both the virtues and the miseries of both worlds. And both the miseries and the virtues of modernity are separable and so are the miseries and virtues of traditionalism, and normally you cannot have it both ways.

Ignatieff: But let me pursue this theme. One of my favourite pieces of your writing is the wonderful press conference with the devil. Years ago you wrote *The Devil's Press Conference* which he might have held had he appeared in Warsaw in 1963, I think it was. And one of the things that you have the devil say in that press conference which has remained in my mind ever since is the sense that one of the greatest losses that followed the decline of religion has been the decline of the idea of the devil itself. And the reason you said that is that modern secular consciousness is particularly helpless in the face of radical evil. And is that one of the weaknesses then of modern humanism, that it can't think about evil?

Kolakowski: Yes, well let's say so. The word humanism has, of course, as you know, many versions, many meanings, but there are two basic meanings which should be distinguished. One meaning of humanism is essentially humanism which consists simply in the view of man as being free, as being able to choose good or evil for himself, as being able to raise himself to the level of angels or sink to the level of animals, and anyway that his dignity consists in that he's able to make a free choice between good and evil. This version is compatible with Christian tradition, I think. Even so, not with all kinds of philosophical traditions of Christianity, but basically it is compatible with Christianity. There is another version, another meaning of humanism, implying that we are free in establishing what is good or evil, that we do not find any ready-made rules of good and evil, good and evil is what we decide freely in this very moment. This version is of course incompatible with Christianity even in the loosest sense. And this humanism which was growing over the last few centuries is, I think, one of the reasons of both our intellectual and moral desires. The idea that there is nothing like good and evil which we find, which can be distinguished according to some ready-made rules, the concept that we produce those rules according to our wishes or whims, this I think is disastrous. Yes, I would defend the idea of the devil as a very important part of our culture, and the loss of which brought us incalculable disaster.

Ignatieff: What about the devil, Octavio Paz?

Paz: Well now, when you think about the devil as absence of motives, well I don't know if it's the devil, what it is is evil. And I think the great poverty of modern thought is the incapacity to think about evil. But of course in some way I have sympathy also with the devil, as, being a poet, I remember William Blake who said that every poet in some way is in connection, is in sympathy with evil, with the devil.

Ignatieff: Now, what do you think he meant by that?

Paz: I think he was thinking of another thing. He was a gnostic perhaps. He had the idea that the devil was a kind of devil with great energy, and he was repeating the old idea of the gnostics who saw the creator as a real devil. Because he has created this desolation of the world. You see, a very anti-Platonic idea. And then I suppose that was the idea of William Blake referring to Milton.

Ignatieff: But do you feel as a poet that Blakeian idea that to be a poet you have to be very close to those kind of infernal energies?

Paz: Infernal energies that are not diabolic in the sense of religion because they are not negative.

Ignatieff: They are positive.

Paz: They are positive. Yes, in this sense, of course: I think that a poet — not only a poet, every human being — must be in relation with his inner self. And being in relation with his inner self, he's in relation with these creative forces. And not only with rational forces. But again, my position is ambiguous, and religion and poetry are linked, because they depend on the same basic situation. I suppose philosophy is the same. That we are in discourse, feeling in some way as foreigners, finding otherness in the stars, in our neighbourhoods, in our neighbours, and in this glass of water, in everything. We are facing the other and we are facing inside ourselves the other. To see yourself as the others and also to see the stars as the others. But also to see yourself as part of the whole. And that is, I think, the common ground between religion and poetry. The idea that we are others inside of ourselves and also that we are one with the whole universe. I wrote a short poem that I should like you to read now in English about this. An easy poem inspired by the experience of reading a Greek anthology. I found a short poem, it's a short epigram by the great astronomer Ptolemy, and Ptolemy, who was neo-Platonic, wrote a short poem *Seeing a Star*. And in the star he saw a divine soul and the vision of the star gave him the assurance that he was eternal, because his soul was a spark of the divine light. Well, I wrote a poem with the same subject. It's a homage to Ptolemy, but is rather different. I will read it first in Spanish, and then you will read it in English and perhaps it will be a small interlude of poetry in this too serious discussion (reads poem in Spanish).

Ignatieff: (reads) 'I am a man. Little do I last, and the night is enormous. But I look up, the star is right. Unknowing, I understand. I too am written and at this very moment someone spells me out.'

Ignatieff: (to Kolakowski) Octavio Paz has talked about the poet's vocation in relation to religion and religious questions. You, it seems to me, have one of the most poetic of conceptions of the philosopher's vocation and I'm just wondering whether you could speak about the philosopher's vocation as Octavio has spoken of the poet's vocation?

Kolakowski: No, I don't have any precise idea about the vocation of philosophy. Philosophy after all emerged as an opposition to religion. It has always been in an opposition of a sort to religion in spite of the great tradition of Christian philosophy. Philosophy has always suffered an ambiguity that it cannot get rid of. And it is that, on the one hand, it's supposed to seek the truth, on the other hand it's supposed to define what truth is. And in very modern philosophy this ambiguity is expressed either in that philosophy tries to be a branch of science, and then it sinks into irrelevance, or it falls eventually into nihilism. And it's very difficult to find a way which would be nicer. I mean, this ambiguity's probably unremovable from philosophy. And I would say philosophy has, historically speaking, had a special cultural function. People needed to think of the limit realities, so to speak, which has always attracted philosophers and in fact has made the core of metaphysics. And there's always a trap in philosophy. Philosophers try to speak of what they know is really unspeakable. But this urge, this need to repeat those attempts, however unsuccessful they might have been in the past, never disappears, need never disappear. But it makes the philosopher's position chronically and incurably ambiguous.

Ignatieff: (to Paz) To speak of the unspeakable is surely a phrase that you would recognise as being part of your vocation as well.

Paz: Yes, but I find the same ambiguity. Philosophy cannot speak about the unspeakable and poetry tries to speak but doesn't speak really. It's an illusion. That's why poetry is also made of silence. There is nothing explicit in poetry. And perhaps the ambiguity of poetry is different from the ambiguity of philosophy, but nevertheless it's ambiguous also.

Ignatieff: But let's look at the unspeakable, if we can bear it, a little more closely. We were talking about the devil in a rather light way, and we touched at the edge of evil, also in a light way. But this is the unspeakable, the nature of evil. It seems to me one of the things that dwells on the modern conscience is this sense of an evil that remains unfaced and unexplained since at least the second war, if we only take that as the evil we've just begun to awake from. And it seems to me to have produced what many people have described as a kind of apocalyptic mood in our culture. I mean, if I had to hazard why modern culture, despite its prosperity, is so gloomy, it is this constant unresolved encounter with the unspeakable, this constant unresolved encounter with the evil of the last 45 years in the midst of our prosperity, like a worm that gradually destroys the apple. Now, how do we deal with that apocalyptic mood, how do we understand it, but also how do we criticise it? It's not something that we merely want to register as a philosopher, as a poet, it's something with which we wish to engage.

Kolakowski: Well, philosophers in our century have made various attempts to deal with this problem. Some of them, like Heidegger, try to explain the root of our malaise in contemporary culture as the oblivion of the being, the loss of metaphysical experience, metaphysical insight. Huser, another great thinker one generation earlier than Heidegger, believed that our ability to manipulate things and to predict things in the framework of scientific development is gained at the expense of our understanding. That science somehow left the very idea of understanding aside because it is not needed. Some philosophers, like Jaspers — sorry to mention only German-speaking thinkers — believe that this mass society has lost historical consciousness, it is this lack of historical awareness which puts into despair the seemingly liberated masses. There are various strategies how to deal with these problems but I don't think that philosophers are either called or likely to heal the civilization which feels itself sick. They can either express a general feeling of helplessness or try to diagnose it, but civilization has to take care of itself not on the level of philosophical abstractions but rather on the level of general consciousness.

Ignatieff: But, Octavio Paz, you once wrote a sentence which has stayed in my mind: 'every poem is an attempt to reconcile history and poetry for the benefit of poetry', and I had a sense that that was a potential response to my question, which is poetry's struggle to lift men out of history.

Paz: When I was hearing Kolakowski I was thinking of the different answers that poetry and literature have lent to the same question, as different as philosophers, as Jaspers or Heidegger or any other, but I should say that the great difference is that poets and novelists — we should say the word poets because a great novelist is a good poet always — have tried to answer not by making a diagnostic of the malaise of civilisation but by trying to express the malaise of civilisation. That's the important thing. I think that every civilisation is wounded. Every civilisation has been sick and the answers to the sickness of civilisation, the sickness of man, as Freud would say, are his culture, his philosophy, his religion, his poetry etc. Now, in modern times this great emptiness of the Western world has been expressed for the best part in the 'Waste Land' of Eliot or some poems by Valery or Kafka or Celine — all of them — not Valery who is more sceptical — but in the others we find sometimes, a religious substance, for instance in the case of Eliot. Sometimes this religious information is masked through a political affirmation as in Ezra Pound or Neruda, but especially I think all these poets have tried to fill something. I mean desperation, negation, emptiness is one part of the picture. The other is creation, and after all our century, not in the last ten years perhaps, but before in the first part of the 20th century, has been rich in art and in experiments and when we think of emptiness and desperation and the horrors of the concentration camps and the war etc, we have also a paradisiac vision. For instance, a painter like Matisse, it's very strange that in the 20th century there is a painter like Matisse, and that he paints this beautiful vision of reality full of flowers, full of naked women etc. I suppose that in every civilisation you have this duality. If a civilisation is sick but is able to create, it can survive. And we have been surviving through the creations of the poets, the thinking of the philosophers. We are obsessed with technology and science. Well, it's very important, technology and science, but I think the most important things in this century have not been only the discoveries of technology but some paintings, some poems.

Kolakowski: But nevertheless, this civilisation we have lived in for so many centuries, the Christian civilisation, somehow was able to cope with it. It taught people that they cannot expect paradise on earth, that some sufferings and some shortcomings and some difficulties make an inevitable part of life and that we are able to reconcile ourselves with these inevitable defeats we suffer, and not fall into despair. This was possible in a Christian perspective because Christianity used to give people a framework within which inevitable defeats of life are somehow integrated in a meaningful order. Once we have lost this order there is no meaning any longer to be found in our defeats.

Ignatieff: They're just defeats.

Kolakowski: They're just defeats, leading to nothing, compensated by nothing, unredeemable, so to speak. Nothing but a pure suffering. And that is one of the results of rationalism.

Ignatieff: I'm just wondering how each of you look to future attempts to fill what you have described as a void in modern consciousness. What is it that you look forward to or look towards as being a likely scenario for the future?

Kolakowski: I wish I knew. I can't answer this question. I only believe, without having very strong evidence for it, I simply trust that there are some invariants in human nature which will help us in finding a way out. I do believe that the need to have an encompassing world view and meaning-generating picture of the world, that that is a need which cannot be eradicated from culture. And that it keeps reasserting itself, sometimes in grotesque, sometimes in cruel forms. But I don't believe you can just remove it. And I do believe it will reassert itself in the further development of our civilisation. I do believe as well that the need to assert one's own personality, one's own personal life in freedom, in deciding oneself, making choices, that this need as well cannot be eradicated from human consciousness.

Paz: Well, I agree generally speaking, the religious answer will be the only answer. Sometimes in a grotesque way, sometimes in a very crude way, sometimes in a terrible way — as nationalism for instance, or in trying to resurrect the universal brotherhood of mankind. But I am thinking not in general terms, but in terms of for each of us. Then, in this sense, the thing I miss more in this modern world is not the presence of religion but the absence of philosophical wisdom. Or perhaps the adjective philosophic is not so exact, I should say wisdom. As the old wisdom of the ancients and historics or the Epicurians or the neo-Platonics. We need a new wisdom. And I should say that this new wisdom would be very old because it will be a reconciliation with the oldest parts of us and will be founded, must be founded, not only in reason but also in some kind of poetics. Not poetry, poetics. When I talk about poetics, I am talking about knowledge or recognition of the dark side of us, the tragic side of us. We must face life thinking that we are mortal, that we are going to die, that we are in love and that this love also is mortal. I mean to be again, to see our destiny not with this kind of frivolity that we see it now. In this sense I think we need a new wisdom.

Ignatieff: This is where we'll end tonight. We began with utopia, which could be defined as the human attempt to transcend the tragedy of the human situation, the fact that we die, the fact that we suffer, the fact that we inflict needless, motiveless suffering on each other. It seems to me we've been listening tonight to two men, Leszek Kolakowski and Octavio Paz, who've managed to vindicate the possibility of writing works of beauty and power in a confrontation with the tragic situation of human beings.

CHAPTER 7

Living in the Interregnum

Michael Ignatieff
Johan Galtung, Anthony Giddens and Immanuel Wallerstein

Ignatieff: Over the past six weeks we've been trying to chart the new landscape of modernity — a new politics, a new post-industrial economy, new kinds of personal and cultural identity. Our discussions have been dominated by a sense of living in a time of crisis. For some this is a time of despair, a moment of impasse, when all the old answers, the old dreams, seem to have failed. But others have spoken with exhilaration about living at the edge of a new time. A cynic might ask at this point 'so what's new? Crisis is the very hallmark of modernity. The times are always changing.' So what we need to know is whether we're living through a time of transition, or whether we might even be at the end of the modern era itself. Is this just another crisis or one of the watersheds of history? To put our times in historical perspective, I have with me a European, an American and an Englishman, all with very different views of what we're living through: Johan Galtung, Professor of Politics at Princeton, and one of that rare breed, a historian who's not afraid to ask where we are in the light of 2500 years of history; Immanuel Wallerstein, Director of the Fernand Braudel Centre in New York, who argues that we're living through a 100-year period of economic transformation; and Anthony Giddens, Professor of Sociology at Cambridge, who in a dozen books since the early seventies has called for a radically new way of making sense of modernity and social change. Johan Galtung, if crisis is endemic to modernity, what is it if anything that distinguishes the crisis of the postwar, and particularly post-1973 era?

Galtung: Difficult to say of course. It's a big question. But maybe I would say a kind of feeling that we're hitting the ceiling. Let me just do something very quickly on it. If you look at nature, it's obvious that there are some kind of limits to how much we can go on exploiting nature. We have the phenomena of pollution and depletion. We can postpone it, we can change it from one type of pollution to another, but there are limits. If we look at human beings, I wonder whether our rates of mental disorder are not too high, and our rates of alienation, the feeling of meaninglessness. Our materialist individualism — or individualist materialism — has come to a point where too many people just wonder what the whole thing is about. And in that connection I also wonder whether we are not in a situation where we are generating new types of diseases. I wonder, for instance, whether AIDS is a phenomenon we really have come to grips with, and whether that is not also a sign that we're hitting the ceiling. Take our social formations: very top heavy.

Ignatieff: What do you mean by top heavy?

Galtung: That they are characterised by the three pillars of modernity: bureaucracy, corporation and intelligentsia. The state, capital, and all the academics that are around. Most of them who have sold their capacity as free intellectuals and have become intelligentsia at the service of the state or the capital. And then finally, fourth, if you look at the world system — you are focusing, I think, your question to some extent on the West, on what we often call the first world — well we live in a different world now, a stalemate with the second socialist world, a kind of nuclear suicide pact with the hope that it is a bluff. An almost hopeless relation to the Third World, as if we are condemned to intervene, to continue trying to repress them in one way or the other. And they of course responding in this phase of neo-colonialism with the weapons of the weak: fundamentalist religion and terrorism. And then finally, to top it all, what I call the fourth world: the East and South-East Asian countries, headed by Japan, with a tremendous economic challenge, simply able, it seems, to make products of better quality at lower prices and simply out-compete us. Now add up all of that and I would say you get a sense of crisis.

Ignatieff: That's a list of symptoms. Immanuel Wallerstein can we look a little at causes? You're a man who specialises in the deep economic causation of modernity in the capitalist world system, how would you situate the current crisis, particularly in its economic dimension?

Wallerstein: Well, I think first of all a preface has to be on the word 'crisis'. That is, it's used for two very different phenomena. When you said crisis is endemic to capitalism you were using it in the sense of economic stagnation, and yes, that's endemic. That is to say we've gone through regular ups and downs of expansion-stagnation for four or five hundred years. Capitalism is built on certain principles that make that inevitable. That doesn't seem to me to be what you really mean. What you really mean is, is there a very special kind of crisis now, a different kind of crisis, one that's calling into question the structure of the system as such? And yes, I would say there is. I don't think that's a crisis of the last 10 or 15 years, that's a crisis that I trace to at least the beginning of the 20th century and would go on at least for 100 to 150 years. And I do think that Johan Galtung's initial capsule phrase that the system is reaching its limits is correct. I think it's reaching its limits in many many ways. I think you have to think of capitalism as a system which is not as it is described either by Adam Smith or Karl Marx. That is to say, everything that we define as capitalism is a sort of asymptote towards which the system has been moving, and were it to get there could not function. That is the full commodification of everything, which is the basic principle of capitalism, has never been achieved. It's a steady upward curve. We have been commodifying more and more and more things —

Ignatieff: Let me come in quickly. 'Commodification' — tell us what you mean.

Wallerstein: Oh well, very simply you take any phenomenon that is useful in the world and you make it a product for purchase and for sale. Cooking, right? Drinking water, that's not yet quite commodified.

Giddens: It's coming.

Wallerstein: It's coming. Breathing air.

Giddens: Perrier air is next in line.

Wallerstein: It's also coming. But obviously all the things that we do buy and sell in the world, including labour. But if you look at capitalism as a historical system, in fact it's the partial commodification of everything which has made it function, and its internal contradiction is that to solve the short-run problems it commodifies more. And the limit which it is reaching, I think, is that we're coming close to or reaching the relatively full commodification of everything, and at that point the system is in crisis, can't function, because it can't in fact guarantee the further accumulation of capital. It's like an asymptote.

Ignatieff: Okay, Before I bring in Anthony Giddens on this, you trace the origins of the current crisis to the beginning of the 20th century, could you amplify on that?

Wallerstein: Well, I think the economic trends which I've been adverting to, which could be matched by various kinds of political trends, were beginning to come to a high enough point of the scale. One of the things that they bred as part of their process are what I call anti-systemic movements which took, historically, two principal forms — the socialist movements and the nationalist movements — and they now have taken many, many more forms, which movements are themselves products of the capitalist world system and are themselves suffused with its contradictions. Nonetheless, they have begun to become more and more and more important in the system, thus creating the political challenge to the survival of the system, combined with — and this is very important to note — the continued success of the system. The system has been marvellously successful economically, that's what happened between 1945 and roughly '67. It never expanded as magnificently as then, and I personally would predict that, come 1990 or 1995, we're going to have another phase of absolutely extraordinary expansion which will put the last one in the shadow. Nevertheless, that very process is further polarisation of the world's populations both socially and economically and is pushing the system towards its limit. So the very success of capitalism will come to an end, not because it fails, but because it succeeds, is the basic message.

Ignatieff: Okay. Tony Giddens, we've had capitalism and modernity pretty well equated, that is, Immanuel Wallerstein has made capitalism the driving wheel of modernity. Now, do you buy that account?

Giddens: Well, what I see is first of all a need to revise our ways of looking at these phenomena, that is, to break away from the unidimensional picture. I just don't think the modern world is created by capitalism. I think modernity has been created by capitalism plus other influences. I therefore don't think it will go away if and when capitalism goes away. I think this means revising some of our traditional political and social theories. For example, I don't think it's conceivable that the advent of socialism in any version, whether it's state socialism or some version that Professor Wallerstein might have in mind, is going necessarily to change the whole series of parameters of what it's like living in a modern society. I think this is true of, for example, ecological movements. That's why I would distinguish industrialism from capitalism. I think it's true of feminism. I think it's true of a whole range of institutions that aren't captured by simply the notion of the expansion of the world capitalist economy. I don't really think that they're captured by the idea of a global logic of the West, because in that respect I think I have more sympathy with Professor Wallerstein's position. That is, that there was a fundamental set of discontinuities that ripped the West away from what went before, and these date from somewhere around the 16th century or so.

Galtung: Well at that point let me just say what my view is.

Ignatieff: Since it's being so misinterpreted.

Galtung: Because maybe I'm entitled — since you have been kind enough to tell me what it is — maybe I could participate at least. My view, in very simple terms, is that in the Greek or Roman period we were steered, or they were steered, by a highly expansionist logic which hit the ceiling. We got the decline and the fall of the Western Roman empire. The Eastern Roman empire had a particular trick which made it possible to continue for a long time. It's a very interesting thing. And at that point a change of logic took place, or cosmology or code, or what you want. And I see what is often called the Middle Ages, which incidentally I think I would date from roughly 300 to roughly 1300, with the Black Death as the *coup de grace*. And then you have a transition period and a new period of expansion. So expansion, contraction, expansion. Now, according to that kind of thinking, of course I do think that we're heading for a period of contraction. And of course I also do think that much of the logic of what today passes for the Green movement is a precursor of that. There are two elements. So let us now look at them. One of them would be a more localised, decentralised type of society, closer to nature, and it would be much less concerned with economic growth. You see, if at some point the system somehow no longer goes in for economic growth, then I will say that some transformation has taken place, even if there is still buying and selling of means of production. Second, I think that a country that decides that its security is better taken care of by entirely defensive means of defence than those horrendous offensive means of defence ending with weapons of mass destruction that we have, ultimately ending with SDI, is a country which at least is not less secure than those countries that go in for nuclear arms. So here we are in the midst of it. We are in the midst of the transition, and a major part of that transition is to my mind the advent of women into politics in a fashion we have never seen before. So take the ecological movement, the feminist movement, the peace movement, the Green movement as an umbrella over it, and we have an example of things going on. And you have both relatively concrete visions, some of them tentatively implemented, some of them on the way. Now, I think it'll take generations to work this out, but you cannot say that it is vague. It's going on right now and the system hates it. They know perfectly well, the Blue know perfectly well that the enemies are no longer the Red, but the Green.

Ignatieff: Anthony Giddens, you look sceptical to me.

Giddens: Yes, I'm sceptical of that sort of scenario, and I'm sceptical of the confidence — perhaps there isn't a confidence with which it's stated.

Galtung: It's the task of a Briton to be sceptical, that's why we have the British.

Giddens: I do think that there are two deeply-rooted elements of why we all feel uncertain. One is, I think, how we handle time and how we handle the application of knowledge to time. I think one could say that from the Enlightenment until something like the turn of the 20th century it was thought we could use knowledge of society to shape the course of our social development. And this gave us a kind of linear backup into time, and a linear progression into the future. I think we now know that isn't so. We develop more and more knowledge about the social world and we use that knowledge to change the social world, but it doesn't allow us to control it. Not in a simple sense. It detaches us from that kind of simple movement from one point to another, and that's what creates this kind of lurching feeling. I think that is the best metaphor to describe the feeling of modernity now — the erratic coursing into the future in which futurology is an integral part of what the future is. Because we use information so much to regularise what we do that we're constantly thinking about what the future might be. Therefore there is no end. There is no possibility of avoiding futurology, but it doesn't produce a precise and predictable future. It produces this lurching, careering, tumbleweed kind of process, which is very different I think from the 19th century view. Could I just add one more thing? I think that the backdrop to that as well is nuclear war, is the fact of the progression of the trend of the industrialisation of war to a situation where war now can destroy the whole of humanity. No one else has had to live against that backdrop. We're the first individuals whose lives might terminate with the end of the life of the whole of humanity. No one else has had to live with that sense of contingency. And I still find evolutionary style thinking tends to have a trust in the capability of avoiding war which is probably misplaced.

Wallerstein: Can I try to systematise lurching — I think his lurching is more systematic than he's giving it credit — and disagree in the course of that a little bit with Johan Galtung? It seems to me you have to think of anti-systemic movements, as I said, emerging in the 19th century. All right, what were they? They were these socialist, nationalist movements. In Johan Galtung's three worlds — I don't think his fourth world is a separate world — but in his three worlds, his standard three worlds, the Western world, the communist world or socialist bloc or whatever, and the Third World, we have had a story which is insufficiently celebrated of the remarkable success of the anti-systemic movements. What success? That is to say, all these movements of the 19th century made a kind of a strategic decision. They were going to transform the world towards a more egalitarian world by obtaining state power. And in fact in the West the social democratic parties basically have come to state power. In the East the Third International has come to state power. And in the Third World the nationalist movements have come to state power. There are a few countries where they haven't, but basically 90 per cent. And the point is they haven't transformed the world. Which is part of the crisis of all these movements. That is, they're suddenly aware that achieving state power did not transform the world. Now I think what you get is a triple set of additional movements. In the Western world, as a reaction to social democracy, you get all the movements that Johan Galtung's been describing.

Ignatieff: Why are they reactions to social democracy?

Wallerstein: To the belief that by achieving state power through the standard group of workers, through the ballot box etc, and adding a government you would change the world. And in fact the ecologists say 'nonsense', the feminists say 'nonsense', the peace movement says 'nonsense', and they're all of course involved in enormous fights with the trade unions and the social democratic parties etc, etc.

Galtung: Above all, to capitalism, much more.

Wallerstein: Well, yes, but to social democracy as a way of fighting the capitalist system.

Giddens: Isn't there also the thing, part of the discovery of modernity is multi-dimensional?

Wallerstein: Well, fine, but also they are concerned with how you transform the world. And they are reacting to the assertion that the achievement of state power will do it. In the Eastern world you in fact have a series of movements that have emerged, which we could trace through Hungary and Poland and China and so forth and so on, which have no good name but they're anti-bureaucratic movements of a multiple kind and which seem to me a reaction to the Third International ideology of how you transform the world. And we are beginning to see in the Third World now a whole series of movements emerge which are reactions to the nationalist movements, again. So what I think you have now, as I see it, are six kinds of movements floating round the world, each of them relates to the other five, if you look at their statements, by criticising the other five. No one of them likes any one of the other five basically.

Ignatieff: Let's list them.

Wallerstein: Well, the so-called new social movements in the Western world versus the old social democratic movements. The communist parties in power in the Eastern world versus the Solidarity, Cultural Revolution, what you will, humanist communism etc in the Eastern world. The nationalist movements in power in the Third World, plus — again there's no good name for all these new movements that are emerging — some of the religious movements, fundamentalist movements, in fact have this great flavour of rejecting the nationalist ideology as a Western liberal solution etc. So you have six sets of movements and each of them, if you look, will tell you what's wrong with the other five. My personal view is all six are right about each other. And the issue now is going to be whether in the next 50 years, 20 to 30 years even, a new great debate among those who wish to transform the world in a relatively egalitarian democratic direction about the strategy, comparable to the debate I see having taken place in Europe from 1850 to 1880, will in fact take place and will come out with some new strategy. I'm not convinced that the Greens have this new strategy. I'm convinced they're looking for it, but I'm not convinced they have it.

Ignatieff: What seems clear enough, if this is a moment to summarise, is that faced with a crisis in modernity it seems clear from everything that's been said that our politics, the agenda of existing social democratic parties, nationalist movements, perhaps even polemically ecological movements, none of them have succeeded somehow in grasping the systemic character of the crisis that you're sketching out.

Wallerstein: I believe that, I would accept that.

Giddens: I believe and I don't believe it. That is, I believe that in some sense there isn't this systematic character. There isn't a single crisis and there isn't a single system. Not in the same sense as Immanuel Wallerstein thinks there is. And what in some part these movements have grasped, I think, and what modern political debates have grasped, is the complexity of the various dimensions of civil society which can't necessarily be transformed through politics, and the dimensions of politics which can't necessarily be transformed through economics. So, for example, I don't think it follows that the debate over the position of women in modern societies can be resolved from an anti-capitalist movement. I don't think that those two things are simply aspects of the same thing. So this is a discovery, I think, to political theory which has been obsessed with capitalism and socialism.

Ignatieff: But it must be a matter of some astonishment, surely, that if we're defining the political actors who will effect these transitions to the post-modern world, or whatever the future is, that in our list of those actors we've not included the Grenadier Guards of the old social struggles? That is, the unions, the parties, the class parties. I'm just wondering why.

Wallerstein: I don't exclude them.

Ignatieff: You don't? But I sense that Johan Galtung would.

Wallerstein: That's right, and I'm disagreeing with him because he's putting his eggs in one of the six baskets that are around and I'm saying that what I see as important is that the six actors, which are the six varieties of movements, in fact engage in some kind of massive dialogue over a 30 year period to come — and I don't know how it'll come out — to come up with a strategy which will be efficacious in transforming the world in the direction that they all claim. Hypothetically, they all claim they're moving in the same direction more or less.

Ignatieff: But what if Tony Giddens is right, that there isn't one crisis? So the sense that six different social actors are going to come together on a common kind of sense —

Wallerstein: Oh I don't know that they are. I said it's important that they debate it. I don't know they're going to come together.

Giddens: But I think the situation can be understood actually, because there are two things going on, as I would see it, in relation to social movements. One is a detachment from the view that it is the economy which is fundamentally the transformative force which changes everything, so if you change the economy through politics you can thereby move towards changing all the major institutions, whereby one would produce the good and true society. The second thing, I think, is that social movements are the other side of the organised character of the modern world, the other side of the organisation of knowledge for the control of the conditions of our lives, day to day social lives. Social movements therefore are bound to spring up in the areas Johan Galtung has mentioned because they're part of the application of knowledge to the transformation of the world.

Wallerstein: Absolutely, I don't disagree with any of that. I've never said that if you change the economy everything else changes. I've said that it's an integrated whole and you can't change one chunk *a* and then it affects *b*. I say you can't even begin to think about it that way. It's exactly the way the Second and Third International did think about it. You nationalise the means of production and everything follows therefrom. And I don't agree, of course.

Giddens: Well there are systems around where they're much more loosely articulated than you think they are.

Ignatieff: Surely what we're directing here is a criticism, you've called it Third International kind of politics but —

Wallerstein: Second and Third.

Ignatieff: But let's enlarge it. What we're talking about is the bankruptcy of a socialism which tied a social diagnosis to the conquest of state power, to a sense that the economic was determinant, and to the sense that political action was sufficient. And we're faced with a whole new set of social actors who clearly are faced with the consciousness that that way of conducting politics has failed.

Wallerstein: Bankruptcy overstates it for me.

Ignatieff: Great difficulty.

Wallerstein: Yes, certainly.

Ignatieff: Let's get whatever agreement we can here.

Galtung: Let me jump into that one, because I think that's a fascinating problem, and I think it's a little bit too crude to put the trade unions on the other side, if you will. I think it depends — in my experience, since I've been working quite a lot on it and in it — depends on what kind of trade union. There is one in the heavy industries in Germany, the biggest trade union in Western Europe, they would tend to be, I think, to some extent for the status quo, in the sense of maintaining heavy industries. Of course, that's what gives them work, their hope being for a German expansionism in the Third World, while not being very much concerned with what happens in the Third World country where that expansionism takes place, and being worried about the ecological criticism from the smokestacks. But if you now take a lot of other workers in other industries, you don't necessarily find that attitude. So you can get both kinds of things, you see, and a contradiction is here to work on. But at that point I have a disagreement with Wallerstein about his model of the six baskets. If you take the alternative movements in the first world and you take the new liberation movements in the Third World and you take the human rights movements in the second world, they have quite a lot in common. There was a fascinating conference in Malta last year bringing together exactly those movements. Heaven knows, it was difficult to establish a dialogue.

Ignatieff: But what is the point of commonality?

Galtung: The point of commonality is a common reaction to the bigness of state and capital. The bigness. You find it in the alternative movement in the West, the human rights movement in the East, and you find it in all those small minorities that have been sort of steamrolled over in the Third World. And that reaction to bigness is a common theme. Whereas on the other hand, the three other baskets, to my mind, are socialised into the Western cosmology, the Western way of seeing it. Here there is a distinction — you people talk about the crisis of the world, I talk about the crisis of Western civilisation.

Ignatieff: Johan Galtung, one of the limits that we seem to be hitting, to adopt the terminology you've been using is the very viability of Western cosmology. That is, Western faith in science, Western faith in reason. And yet the critique of Western faith in science and reason often is sustained by an irrationalism of its own kind. What kind of rational critique can you make of Western rationalism?

Galtung: Well, you've put your finger just right on my problem personally. Being a part of the West and being a part of Western rationality, how can I stand outside that and criticise it? But I can try to formulate it in some formulas. I think that Aristotle and Descartes in two different periods are names that can serve as pegs on which we can hang two important aspects of the Western way of thinking. Atomism, that we take vast phenomena and subdivide them into sub-phenomena, and then we try to take them one at a time. According to Descartes we should start with the easier ones.

And the second one: deductivism. We make statements about those atoms that we have singled out and then we try to chain those statements together in a deductive system which is more or less pyramidal and more or less elegant. The French when they formulate it make it very elegant — and of course it has to be said in French — and the Germans when they formulate it make it very deductive, and perhaps not so elegant — and the German language is good for that one. The British have a tendency to like neither one nor the other, but to stay with very small pyramids so as to avoid what in Britain is called sweeping generalisations. But the basic point being this element of atomism and deductivism as opposed to holism and dialectics.

Ignatieff: Holism? Define your terms.

Galtung: Okay. Trying to see totalities. One way of trying to say what that may be similar to is called interdisciplinary, transdisciplinary approaches, I'm not saying it's exactly the same but it is in that direction. At least you wouldn't go in for economic determinism if you think that you will try a holistic approach. They are the wrong dialectics. But the logic that steers this phenomena, the forces and counter forces and processes and transcendencies and new systems and things of that kind, that deductive thinking tends to steer you into too rigid systems that don't have enough flexibility to reflect these tremendous changes that we see in the real world.

Ignatieff: Well, we are prisoners of our own thinking. We seem to have got in fact into what could be described in another term as the crisis of social science, which in common language is a crisis in the very language we use to understand social phenomena. Now, how do you live or experience this sense that we are prisoners of our own thinking?

Giddens: Well, two themes I think I would address in that really. One is that I would describe the crisis of modernity intellectually, the transition from modernity to post modernity, as being bound up with the discovery that reason does not create rationality. That is, that the application of scientific reason, whether natural scientific reason or social scientific reason, to try to change the world does not allow us simply to control it and project it along a pre-given path of development. That's the erratic character of modernity I described earlier and I think it's bound up with that discovery. That is, although we understand the world better it doesn't allow us to shape it better necessarily because all sorts of unintended consequences occur which channel it away from what we intended when we produced certain changes. That discovery is fundamental.

Ignatieff: Can you give us an example of that startling statement that the use of reason does not lead to rationality?

Giddens: Yes, I think it's true of science itself because I think the predominant ethos of science, of natural science, used to be that natural science is the epitome of reason, that it therefore leads to a better world. That scientific developments produce other forms of progress, and that those are correlated. We know, in an era of nuclear weaponry, that that is not true. We know that science is a double-edged phenomenon at best. And we know this too, I think, of all forms of the application of rational knowledge to attempts to change the world.

Ignatieff: But the critique of Western science, indeed the critique of Western reason, the sense that rational means produce irrational ends, has now become a kind of cliche of our sense of what's wrong with the current world. What kind of valid rational critique of science can we get? I mean, I'm confused as a result of what I've heard here.

Giddens: It's not that reason produces irrationality, it's that the application of reason doesn't produce technological control of the world in which we live that allows us to control that world in a uni-directional fashion. The implication of that for social science, I think, is that social scientists used to think that they could get to know the social world better and that therefore we could control it better.

Ignatieff: A critic would say that's exactly the kind of core value of Western modernity that's got us into trouble. Control in the sense of scientific mastery of nature, domination of nature, domination of other people. That is, how do you distinguish between control and domination, and what in fact do you mean by control?

Giddens: Well, by control I mean simply in the context in which I used it, the capability of guiding the world, of guiding events in the world, whether these be social events or natural events. I think it is true that the attempt to control the world has undercut some of the basic ways in which one would like to see ourselves live life. I think there's a lot of truth in the idea that modern society undercuts the basis of its own moral legitimation. That is to say, for example, we don't really have morally viable ways of handling sickness, death, existential crises of life, because they're undercut by the very nature of the world in which we live, which is based on the idea of technology and control. I don't mean just that though. I mean that we've come to see that we don't control the world in the way in which that scenario would suggest. So it's not just that it rips away the moral fabric of the basis of day-to-day life, it's also that it was a misapplied metaphor of control because the world remains erratic, the world remains out of our control in fundamental ways. The problem with the modern world is not that it's a bureaucratically controlled phenomenon, it's not the Weberian phenomenon of a tightly knit rationalised 1984-like world, it's a world which is out of control in substantial ways through our attempts to control it.

Wallerstein: The interesting thing is that this crisis is being felt in the physical sciences today. And you have people within the physical sciences, albeit still a minority, who are talking about the arrow of time, who are challenging Newtonian principles, who are talking about the basic physical, chemical processes being processes which lead to bifurcations which are not unilinear and in which the object is to explain more and more complex structures and not to simplify complexity into simplicity. This is a terribly important movement. Again, it's a movement of the last 10-20 years, and I trace that as a reflection of the overall crisis of the historical system. The physical sciences were born more or less with the system. The social sciences emerge after the French revolution, because the system has reached a particular stage in which they have to rationally explicate the process of political and economic change which has now become so obvious, and they have done it with categories which reify, which —

Ignatieff: What do you mean by reify?

Wallerstein: They take something, give it a name, and that name then becomes an acting element in the world, the name, the state, the bourgeoisie etc. All losing from consciousness the fact that the very content of that term, the very meaning of the term, the very social reality it reflects is itself a constantly changing phenomenon. And therefore making false comparisons across all time and space without any sense of the structural context. And this goes along with Johan Galtung's sense of the need for holism in dialectics of regarding the processes of the contemporary historical system — that is contemporary for 5-600 years, the one in which we're living — of being a single process, which is a very extraordinary process and in which all our social science has to be the explication of its complexity rather than reducing it to its simplicity.

Ignatieff: Okay. It seems to me, what you've been describing here, is a crisis of knowledge.

Wallerstein: That is correct.

Galtung: Epistemology.

Ignatieff: A sense that we are prisoners of our own ways of thinking. We are prisoners because these ways of thinking are atomistic. They are narrowly deductive. They are enclosed in disciplines which fragment a reality that needs to be seen as a whole. They are excessively abstract, they're not sufficiently historical. Crisis of knowledge. Tony Giddens, though, was referring to something else which takes us into another area, which is a crisis of value. When you talked about Jurgen Habermas's notion that modernity consumes its own moral legitimacy, I had a feeling that you were trying to connect a crisis of knowledge, that is, the emergence of a certain kind of science and a crisis in value. The destruction of a stable, enduring and plausible set of moral relations between people.

Giddens: Yes, I was trying to connect them, because I think they were very much bound up with one another in the period up until at least the First World War. That is, the idea that we could systematically control our environment, control our world, was bound up with a certain moral security in what that world is and should become. And I think the loss of the one in some part does go along with the loss of the other. So that we live in a fragmented world which at the same time, I fully agree, needs to be grasped in a certain sense holistically. And I don't see those as contradictory.

Ignatieff: Let's get a little more specific about what we mean about the crisis of moral legitimacy. It's a phrase that, as the poet says, comes tripping off the tongue, but we need to understand what it really means in practical terms. What about an example here?

Giddens: Yes, I think it would be a good idea to give two examples really. One is the one I was alluding to before. That is, we live day-to-day lives in which for most of what we do we can't give any reason. We dress as we do, we walk around as we do, we appear on TV programmes, these things are part of a tissue of day-to-day social activity which really isn't explained. It's hard to say why we do these things apart from the fact that they're there and we do them. We're bound up in a mechanism of doing them. That I think is very different to how it used to be, what it used to be like living in a traditional social world, a more traditional culture, even, say, an 18th century European culture. There's a very different sense I think of moral lapse there.

Ignatieff: But isn't one of the moral claims of social science precisely that if you can substitute knowledge, rational understanding of the reasons for action, for habit, custom, tradition, religion, you produce what is a more rational society in the good sense? Of human beings who actually know why they're doing what they're doing? And surely that means a legitimate moral world?

Wallerstein: But that leaves something out.

Ignatieff: What?

Wallerstein: It leaves out the element of a hierarchical structure of power within the system. That's even hypothetically. If we all knew exactly what it is we were doing and why we were doing it and understood exactly how all the mechanisms operated, it does not follow, which is a presumption of 18th century Enlightenment thought, that we would all act like Kantian moral men for the good of all beings. We might in fact use it for quite opposite purposes. Or knowing it, we would still be helpless because we are otherwise too weak. Let me give you an important example of the implications of our framework of social science. After 1945 a new major field in the social sciences emerged. It was called development, consequently economic development, social development, political development. This was coming to terms with the Third World, right? There was this Third World out there, we were going to explain it, how it developed. The assumption built into our Enlightenment theory is that if we could understand that then we would all be helping the process of development and speeding it up. We worked on certain universalising theories in which we used false units of analysis, the stages. We developed stages theories — from Rostow's stage theory to Stalin's stage theory, it doesn't matter — in which we assumed that people are in stages one to five or six. And therefore the model of the one who's in stage one should be to look at the model of stage six, and if they would only apply the wisdom and we would send them technical assistance — we the scholars, we the governments — then they would do that. Well, that assumed that in fact if we did that, first of all that they would then all develop along those lines because of the universalising principle. Secondly, that that was our motivation and our interest and so forth. In fact, of course, the crisis is that instead of some sort of convergence occurring, the last 45 years has shown a continuing process — for the last 400 years, but it's been more evident in the last 45 years — of a deepening polarisation of different zones of the world economy which goes right against all development theory, which is why development theory is now an embarrassment of the sixties. But you ask for a specific example of how you can take the concept of universalising laws, translate it into a real analysis of a real social problem, come up with very false conclusions which are then put into practice, not merely by scholars but by governments, and then come up 10-15 years later and say, 'my god, it just doesn't make any sense, it isn't coherent with reality.'

Galtung: The example is perfect and I wonder if I could just bring it a little bit back to what to me is the Western concept of rationality? Because I insist all the time on the civilisational factor here. Let me give one little metaphor from Hindu thought. It's very short. According to Hinduism there are four basic values. They are called wealth and duty and pleasure and liberation, spiritual liberation. Now, any other civilisation could have a similar list. But the Hindu point about it is this: if you pursue only one of these four you will not even get that one. If you want these values, you pursue all four of them with patience at the same time. Now what is typical of Western rationality is uni-dimensionalism, uni-causality, and that is tied in with that pyramid I mentioned, because there is a tendency to confuse the logically antecedent with the factually antecedent. And because the pyramid is neat in our thoughts, reality is supposed to be equally neat.

Wallerstein: That's what I mean by reification.

Galtung: And that is one element of reification and a very important one. Now there is an important factor here which comes in, namely, when we take the Western idea of progress, coupled with a certain impatience and with what I tried to describe as a kind of love-hatred relation to crisis, then exactly by pursuing one of the four we wreak havoc. But before we do that we have some glittering affluence along that line, and that's exactly Wallerstein's point about capitalism destroying itself by succeeding. That's exactly the point. See, here we're back again to your point about physics. And if I may say something, namely that I also find in all these opposition movements, a great distrust of any single factor, the idea that it is not correct, that women are not entitled to say 'you ecologists and you peace people, you wait till we women are in power and we shall take care of that one.' Nor can the peace people say, 'wait with this ecology and women talk, first we have to have peace, we have to get rid of this basic thing and then the women and the ecology can come.' Now, I'm not saying it's equally successful, the idea that there is a multiplicity of factors and it is no longer the Second and Third International faith that if we just get the power of the state we can fix it from there on.

Wallerstein: Complexity is a virtue.

Galtung: Complexity, and better 40 or 20 small steps along 20 dimensions than one big step along one.

Ignatieff: I think you're making a very interesting observation that there's a very deep relationship between the ways we analyse the world and the kinds of political strategies we develop, the deep structures of our thought. If we have one dimensional forms of social analysis we get one dimensional forms of political praxis. That's fine. But I've got a big difficulty with all the discontent with Western rationality, which is simply that I've never seen a critique of Western rationality that didn't reinforce either rationality or that didn't proceed from essentially a deeply irrational revolt from the whole process of reason, of knowledge.

Galtung: Just a second, what is irrational about the revolt, of being offered a choice between dying from cancer and a nuclear war? I mean, there are many of us who like me believe that this is the choice we're offered. And there are good reasons for saying so. We can take the curves and extrapolate them in a very Western way, and there's nothing irrational in saying that not only those two factors, but the multiplicity of factors are ganging up against us because we are reaching the limit.

Wallerstein: But if I may say so, I fear your discomfort with the possibility of total irrationalism is a sort of bounceback — and this combines with the previous discussion about anti-systemic movements — it is in a sense the same kind of problem as the relationship of that first tier of anti-systemic movements with the second tier of anti-systemic movements. But I'm not on one side or the other, I share both their critiques of the other, and I think there has to be a real dialogue here. And I have the same sense in the issue of science as we've known it from Roger Bacon to Francis Bacon to Newton to Einstein. Its fundamentals are up for grabs again. The questions are being reopened. I'm not sure where we come out, any more than I'm sure where we come out with the anti-systemic movements, any more than I'm sure that there'll still be a question where we come out with the end of the capitalist world. What I do say is that we have got to eliminate all the assumptions, go back into all our a prioris and say 'okay let's put them on the table and let's ask questions about them, debate them.' You know, what are units of analysis etc, etc, etc. And I see a 30-50 year process, an intellectual process and a political process — and you can't separate the two — of resolving that issue and maybe we may not resolve it. At the end of 50 years we'll be in utter confusion and so forth, or we may come up with more sensible ways of looking at the world.

Giddens: Why not try and put it a bit more cogently, as I think Michael's quite right, one must defend a certain concept of rationality and I think all of us would accept that, but we probably all would defend a more historicised notion of rationality than the one which —

Ignatieff: What would a historicised notion of rationality mean?

Giddens: I think it's a rolling notion of rationality.

Ignatieff: Rolling?

Giddens: Yes, in the sense in which Popper claims there are no fixed foundations for science but nevertheless science is not irrational. That's a kind of claim, I think, which whatever you think of Popper's own writings, echoes through modern attempts to get to grips with what epistemology could become in the —

Wallerstein: Yes, I like that idea. You see, our epistemology has been an assumption of progress, so that what is today is better than what was yesterday. What was yesterday is better than the day before. Now, one possibility is to take something like Weber's notion of substantive rationality and say that's formal rationality and is probably undoubtedly true in some technicist sense, but let us evaluate the overall whole in terms of what? Well, at that point we come to basic metaphysical questions which have not been terribly popular in Western thought for 4 or 500 years but maybe should become popular again, and we should debate what is the good society.

Ignatieff: A harsh critic would say we've been engaging in a kind of medieval disputation about angels dancing on the head of a pin in the specific sense that we may not have any time — that is, these discussions we have about values, about the good society, are conducted in the 59th minute of the 23rd hour of the human race in a sense.

Wallerstein: 57th minute and we don't have time for anything else, that's my answer.

Ignatieff: That's your answer.

Galtung: And my answer is that that debate is indispensable in order to know how to spend those three minutes.

Giddens: It's more than that, it's part of the shadow of modernity and its transition to post-modernity. I think it's part of the contingency that we now feel about the world and we have to repress it because it's not easy to see how we can cope with it. But I think it's there and that's part of our intellectual culture. And our day-to-day life, I suppose, too.

Ignatieff: What is this post modernity?

Giddens: Well, I think it's the transition we've been discussing. That is, for me it's the rolling nature of reason. It's the interlacing changes we talked about at the beginning of this debate between the various dimensions of modernity, and it's the difficulty of living in a sequential motion of time any more, I think, in which the future is already with us and we have to use it to create that future and so you get this careering path away from the programmed nature of what the Enlightenment version of modernity was all about, I think.

Ignatieff: I think that's where we should end. We've covered a tremendous lot of ground at a very, very high level of altitude. We've talked about the biggest possible words there are: modernity, history, post-modernity. I hope this discussion has vindicated the difficult and unpopular thought that this really is the only level at which a full encounter with the difficulty of our times is adequate.